"Aaron Hurst powerfully sums up in *The Purpose Economy* the fundamental changes taking place in the business world."

Arianna Huffington
Chair, President and Editor-in-Chief
Huffington Post Media Group

The Purpose Economy

How Your Desire for Impact, Personal Growth and Community Is Changing the World

Aaron Hurst

elevate
Elevate, USA

Advance Acclaim

"Here is that rare animal, a business book grounded in compassion. *The Purpose Economy* taps into our deep craving for meaning in our life and work. If Aaron Hurst is right, and I think he is, we are on the threshhold of a new, more value-rich era in business. This book will help you find your place in it."

Daniel H. Pink
Author, To Sell Is Human *and* Drive

"After building the largest nonprofit consultancy in the nation and changing the role of professionals in society, Aaron Hurst takes aim at his next target, the global economy."

Chan Suh
Founder, Agency.com

"Writing with the fierceness and intelligence of one who has been on the front lines of creating the Purpose Economy, Aaron Hurst pulls together a seemingly disparate collection of trends and multi-generational yearnings into a cohesive argument that our economy is entering a new period where meaning is, perhaps, the ultimate capital. *The Purpose Economy* is at once both a description of profound changes and a call to action to make those changes a part of our society."

Jerry Colonna
Chair of the Board, Naropa University | Co-Founder, Flatiron Partners
Author, The Monster in Your Head

"*The Purpose Economy* eloquently sums up what we have seen around the world over the last ten years. Aaron Hurst is a rare visionary with the talent to see the future but also find a way to bring us all along on the journey to realize its potential."

Markus Hipp
Executive Director, BMW Foundation

"*The Purpose Economy* is required reading for anyone interested in social innovation and frankly anyone who is working with Millennials."

Michele Kahane
Professor of Social Innovation and Entrepreneurship, The New School

"Aaron is one of the most thoughtful analysts working at the intersection of business and society interests today. He has a deep, intuitive understanding of people, and the different forces that are affecting their social, economic, and life decisions. If you are interested in understanding where we might be headed and what it might mean for your job, career, or enterprise, you need to read this book."

Stephen Jordan
Founder, U.S. Chamber of Commerce Business Civic Leadership Center

"*The Purpose Economy* is a must-have on any reading list about economics, social innovation, Millennials, marketing, or leadership."

Jim Schorr
Senior Fellow in Social Entrepreneurship
UC Berkeley Haas School of Business

"*The Purpose Economy* is brilliant. It is both an unlock for finding purpose in your career as well as for adapting your organization to meet the shifting priorities of new generations and communities."

Roberto Orci
President, Acento Advertising
Chairman, Association of Hispanic Advertising Agencies

"Aaron Hurst has captured an immensely important change in today's consumer and talent economies. *The Purpose Economy* explains why a growing desire for authentic purpose in the work we do and the choices we make is redefining what it takes to lead successful organizations."

Fabio Rosati
CEO, Elance / oDesk

"For those wondering what's coming around the corner economically and socially—driven by the energy and dynamism of Millennials—*The Purpose Economy* provides some compelling ideas and early clues."

Phillip Henderson
President, Surdna Foundation

"This important book provides important insight into the changing motivations and drive of the powerful Millennial Generation. This thesis can be (and hopefully will be) transformative to a variety of sectors, as we adjust to the new currency of the largest generation in history—Millennials."

Maya Enista Smith
Advisor, Lady Gaga's BORN THIS WAY FOUNDATION

Published in Boise, Idaho by Elevate, a Russell Media company

This book may be purchased in bulk for educational, business, organizational, or promotional use.

For information, please email info@elevatepub.com

ISBN-10: 1937498298
ISBN-13: 978-1937498290

Printed in the United States of America

The Purpose Economy is dedicated
to the amazing women in my family
who have taught me nearly everything I know.
Kara Hartnett Hurst, my muse and wife.
Lola B. Hurst, my daughter
and the closest thing to perfection on this planet.
Tera Pierce, my sister and hero.
Sandra Slater, my rock and aunt.
Bonnie Slater Hurst, my departed mother,
whose disdain for the ordinary lives with me to this day.

Acknowledgements

Robert Acton, Clem Auyeung, Jesse Bania, Caroline Barlerin, Nate Bear, Jonathan Becker, Jennifer Benz, Paula J. Beugen, Ruth Blatt, Sierra Brand, Mischa Byruck, Stuart Bunderson, John Cary, Chris Chavez, Samuel Chen, Arthur Cherry, Josh Cohen, Jerry Colonna, Chip Conley, Alana Corbett, Cody Cowan, Suzanne Craig, Will Denton, Bill Draper III, Leandra Elberger, Jason Elliott, Liana Elliott, Peter Esser, Tatiana Figueiredo, Lindsay Firestone, Lance Fors, Oliver Friedfeld, Kyla Fullenwider, Lisa Gans, Meg Garlinghouse, Sheryle Gillihan, Mirta Gilson, Kimberly Gim, Per Grankvist, Adam Grant, Gabriel Grant, Marine Grodzin, Phi-Hong Ha, Alethea Hanneman, Carol Harnett, Jessica Harris, Meira Harris, R. Christine Hershey, Markus Hipp, Jeff Hirsch, Elizabeth Horwitz, Rachel Hutchinson, Robert Hunter, Shawn Hunter, Noah Isaacs, Luciana Jaburl, Amel Karboul, Meghana Khandekar, Steve Kirmse, Aïcha Konaté, Adriana Krasniansky, Bobby Kuber, Adam Lashinsky, Tracy Lawrence, Chelsea LeMar, Stephanie Lepp, Leonardo Letelier, Julie Lewit-Nirenberg, Josh Linkner, Emily Loose, Christos Makridis, Elaine Mason, David B. McGinty, Denise McMahan, Jeff Nedler, Mark Newall, Frances Nguyen, Joy Nuga, Alexandria Ocasio-Cortez, McVal Osborne, Kelli Peterson, Eric Phillips-Horst, Armin Pialek, Marc Porat, Damon Shelby Porter, Julian Posada, Camille Preston, Tom and Kathy Raffa, Eric Ries, Fabio Rosati, Jeff Russell, Mark Russell, Alexandra Santiago, Frank Santoni, David Sasson, Nina Schneider, Elizabeth Schwan-Rosenwald, Jimena Ryan, Emily Sarver, Steve Schloss, Ryan Scott, Meaghan Scribner, Mariana Serra, Neil Shah, Shally Shanker, Dr. Shikha Sharma, Alex Simon, Aman Singh, Sandra Slater, Adam Spence, Sophie Stenbeck, Jay Arthur Sterrenberg, Wendi Sturgis, Chan Suh, Trevor Sumner, Rich Tafel, Anna Tavis, Michael Thng, Friederike V. Tiesenhausen, Kristy Timms, Jeffery Thompson, Dar Vanderbeck, Gael Van Weyenbergh, Franziska Veh, Jeff Walker, Katherine Wang, Emma White, Arthur Woods, Kristin Woods, Amy Wrzesniewski, Pengcheng Zhu, Andrew Zolli

The Purpose Economy 100

The cover of this book celebrates 100 pioneers of the new economy. Their names are as follows:

Cindy Gallop, David Kelley, Marshall Ganz, Jonathan Trent, Erika Karp, Salman Khan, Michelle Long, Laura Roberts, Emily Pilloton, Antje Danielson and Robin Chase, Yvon Chouinard, Daniel Pink, Howard Gardner, Michael Porter, William McDonough, Brené Brown, Ben Nelson, Wendy Kopp, Sasha Orloff and Jacob Rosenberg, Jonathan Abrams, Dr. Eric Topol, Arianna Huffington, Pam O'Connor, Dr. Peter Tuerk, Greg Berman, Marty Makary & Atul Gawande, William Rosenzweig, Carol Cone, Dr. Corey Keyes, Evan Wolfson, Howard Dean, Heather Franzese, Jeff Denby, Jonathan Rapping, Mary Bonauto, Beth Noveck, Rick Warren, R. Seth Williams, Sebastian Thrun and Peter Norvig, Chad Dickerson and Matt Stinchcomb, Daniel Rosen, Billy Parish, Steve Richmond, Joshua David and Robert Hammond, Joshua Mailman and Wayne Silby, Amy Wrzesniewski and Jane E. Dutton, Rick Fedrizzi, Mike Italiano, and David Gottfried, Jay Coen Gilbert, Bart Houlahan, and Andrew Kassoy, Dr. Melissa Kearney, Dr. Peter Tufano, Dr. Jonathan Guryan, Dr. Erik Hurst, Bob Epstein and Nicole Lederer, Ryan Gravel, Cathy Woolard, Tom Cousins, Ben Cohen and Jerry Greenfield, Craig Jelinek, Bernie Glassman, Juliet Ellis, Freelancers Union, Paul Rice, Charles Montgomery, Jacob Wood & William McNulty, Jennifer Pahlka, Melinda Gates, Jeffrey Stewart, Indra Nooyi, Ryan Howard, Dr. Risa Lavizzo-Mourey, Steve Ells, Ray Oldenburg, Vivek Kundra, Tony Hsieh, Brian Chesky, Joe Gebbia and Nathan Blecharczyk, John Tolva, Rob Spiro and Alon Salant, Yancey Strickler, Charles Adler, Perry Chen, Meg Garlinghouse, Mitchell Baker, Dr. Tom X. Lee, Elon Musk, Peter Koechley & Eli Pariser, David Payne and Michael Tavani, Michael Bloomberg, Rachel Kleinfeld, John Mackey, Michael Pollan, Brad Neuberg, Chris Anderson, David Edinger, Scotty Martin, Dr. Regina Benjamin, Frank Perez, Al Gore, Zack Exley and Judith Freeman, Ben Goldhirsh, Adam Grant, David Javerbaum, Dr. Jon Kingsdale, Jane Jacobs, Jimmy Wales and Larry Sanger, Jorge Montalvo, Judge Jonathan Lippman, Justin Hall, Molla S. Donaldson, Karl D. Yordy, Kathleen N. Lohr, and Neal A. Vanselow, Peter Block

Table of Contents

There are developments in every industry and city that look unrelated up close, but that reveal a pattern when looked at from a distance. They are all connected to creating purpose for people. They represent a new economic era that is driven by the three types of purpose we seek in our lives.

There have been three major economic eras in history: agrarian, industrial, and information. We are now seeing the rise of the fourth era—one based on creating purpose for people.

Social, political, environmental, and business changes are combining at this moment in history to give rise to the Purpose Economy. The ten drivers not only explain the new economy, but also provide insight into how it will take shape.

When it comes to happiness and well-being, what matters most is purpose. Given the amount of time we spend at work, it is in our careers that we should primarily focus our pursuit of purpose.

Most of what we know about purpose is wrong. New research over the last decade is helping us understand what really generates purpose, and this knowledge will change the foundation of how we think about our careers and lives.

Introduction

I am 39 years old. As an American male, my life expectancy is 76. I'm already in the second half of my life, though I'm often still referred to as a "young leader."

It's remarkable how much the world can change in 39 years. Most nations are less than 75 years old. The average national constitution has a life expectancy of only 17 years. The lifespan of a Fortune 500 company is between 40 and 50 years—roughly the same as someone in one of the ten poorest countries in the world. During my grandmother's lifespan, the number of nations in the world increased by more than 50 percent; at the time of her birth, many had not yet even been established.

Our institutions, our governments, and even our nations are still radically evolving. You will likely live longer than the organization that employs you today. The corporations that dominate society are a relatively recent invention, barely a hundred years old. The sector is still in its infancy, and the giant businesses that lead it, despite all their resources and systems, are far less resilient than people. As the founder of the Taproot Foundation, now in its twelfth year, it's hard for me to fathom a time when it won't exist, but the odds are very low that it will still be around when I die. Hopefully its impact and legacy will outlive me, but the organization is unlikely to do so.

It's a disturbing but liberating thought—everything is in transition and far less permanent than we imagine. But if little of what we build or experience outlasts us, we can and should give ourselves far more permission to experiment and take risks. Few things cannot change. That means that we possess much more power than we realize, but it also means that even if we make mistakes, they are impermanent and reparable. Things are done a certain way, until they aren't. You can be the one who makes the change.

Playing with Post-it Notes

In 1992, I was in high school while my father was a Ph.D. student at the University of Michigan. My fondest memory of that time was watching him map his ideas for his dissertation. He began with an insight from a conversation, research, or a book. He then would roll these giant sheets of paper out across the table, on which he would jot down the insight and circle it. He added circle after circle, drawing lines to show their relationships. When he wasn't around, I would pull out his maps and look at them, trying to decipher his lines, words, and circles—it was a map of his mental world, and looking at it made me feel like I was inside it.

20 years later, I began creating my own circles to find my own insights. My circles took the form of Post-it notes stuck on my office window, which overlooked the downtown New York City skyline. For over a year I arranged and rearranged them, trying to find a pattern and an answer to a question I had been studying for a long time: Is there a science to social impact? How could the work I was doing at Taproot have a bigger impact? Billions of dollars are spent each year trying to move the needle on issues from education to poverty, but what was working? Is it possible to predict success? How could someone design a social impact effort with a high probability of creating change?

The breakthrough came as patterns emerged between the Post-its. The patterns became what I later termed the Five Levers for Social Change in a series for the *Stanford Social Innovation Review*.[1] Based on my research of successful social change efforts, there appeared to be only five ways that social change was ever proactively created: research, policy, public perceptions, disruptive technology, and bright spots. This framework radically shrunk the challenge of architecting social change efforts. What had seemed infinite and overwhelming had become finite and easily navigated.

Once this framework emerged, I took it on the road to see if anyone could break it.

Entrepreneurs, local foundations, even folks at the White House couldn't find an example of a social change that had been created using an approach other than one of the five levers. But as I continued to test the framework, I personally found that the five levers weren't enough. Putting the levers to work required large groups of people working together across sectors, backgrounds, and experiences. Leaders weren't listening to each other or respecting the perspectives of their partners. They were talking at each other, not with each other. They were getting stuck just defining an issue, much less selecting the right levers to pull.

Soon, a new set of Post-it notes began to pop up on my window. Why did such smart people see issues so differently and have so much trouble understanding the perspectives of their peers? How could we get people to work together to put the five levers into action? The answer took about three months to emerge as I moved my Post-it notes around in between conference calls and meetings. As I mapped out all the diverse approaches to advancing progress, five distinct perspectives emerged. I came to understand that these diverse perspectives constituted the core of not only how people created change and progress in the world, but also how they experienced purpose in their lives and careers. These perspectives embodied a new kind of diversity, a diversity of purpose.

Purpose Is a Verb

Like so many people, I always thought that gaining purpose in life was about finding my cause. When coaching or mentoring people over the years, purpose always seemed to find expression through a noun—immigration, civil rights, education and so on. And yet this never accurately described the many people I knew who worked in jobs that had no "cause" but still felt a strong sense of purpose in their work, or others who had found purpose working across many causes. What started to become clear to me was that defining personal purpose wasn't about finding a noun, but instead about finding a verb—an action. It's not only what you are doing, but how you do it and thereby relate to the world. For example, when we assemble a group of leaders in education, we think they share a purpose, but in fact, they only share a cause. Until they can understand the diversity of purpose in the room, the cause has little hope of moving forward or creating meaningful change.

This insight led to a third question and set of Post-it notes. What is purpose? What generates purpose for people, and how can they harness it? And perhaps most importantly, how do we engage people to use their purpose to create meaningful change?

This one was easy at first. For more than a decade, Taproot had helped thousands of people find and cultivate purpose. Reading over 20 thousand application essays had provided me with enormous amounts of data, anecdotes, and stories to move to Post-it notes and find the eventual patterns and insights around the drivers of purpose. This time, the magic number was three: people gain purpose when they grow personally, when they establish meaningful relationships, and when they are in service to something greater than themselves.

The harder part was answering the follow up questions about how to enable people to have work rich in purpose. Upon further examination, however, it became clear that for many people, living with purpose was a necessity, not an option. This especially rang true with the Millennial generation. People were seeking and finding purpose everywhere and in everything. It was in businesses like Etsy, who became wildly successful. It was in models and new markets for things like car sharing, and at the core of the rise and success of social media. It was why so many people were deciding to leave their jobs and work for themselves.

It was during this time that I came across a summary of my uncle Marc Porat's work from when he was a doctoral student in economics at Stanford. In his 1977 thesis, he coined the term "Information Economy," and he proved that information had surpassed industry as the leading driver of the U.S. gross domestic product (GDP). In reading the summary of his dissertation, I found something surprisingly similar about what he had described and what I was witnessing both through my work at Taproot and in the economy at large. Specifically, the economy was going through another major restructuring, and that just as the Information Economy supplanted the Industrial Economy, and as the Industrial Economy supplanted the Agrarian Economy before it, a new economy had begun to emerge.

Like most people, I had come to see technology as synonymous with innovation, jobs, growth, and our future. And while the Information Economy was clearly still the dominant driver of our economic engine, it had become clear to me that a new economy was emerging, one centered on the need for individuals to find purpose in their work and lives. It wasn't a pollyannaish vision of the future, but rather a natural course in the evolution of the needs of people and the goods, services and jobs they desired. As I began to share this idea of an emerging Purpose Economy with my friends, partners, and colleagues, it resonated with much of what they had experienced and witnessed in their own work and lives. It wasn't just a trend or niche; as consumers, employers, community leaders, policy makers and employees, we were each playing a small role in restructuring society and the economy to meet the growing demands of the people (and planet).

Of course, the desire for purpose in life is not new; one could argue that it is a core part of the human makeup, a crucial component of what has driven us as a species. But what did this mean? What changes could we expect to see? How could we help nudge the economy in the direction that would be most beneficial to people and the planet? The Information Economy changed organizations and the labor market as well as demanding a new, enabling environment. Could we expect the same types of changes in the emerging Purpose Economy?

The impact of the Information Economy cannot be overstated. Its rise led to radical changes in government, policy, education, community dynamics, non-market human interactions, and the role and design of nonprofit organizations. Within organizations, the Information Economy not only created technology departments, it also catalyzed the widespread introduction of strategic planning, marketing, and human resources. Additionally, it completely altered the flow of capital and investments, accelerating both but also creating a culture that focused on debt, scale, and short-term investment horizons.

Could we expect to see similar radical changes in organizations over the next 20 years? Would whole new functions be invented? In 50 years, would a company even resemble the typical business of today? The clues could be found in studying organizations like the Taproot Foundation and other pioneers working on the front lines of the new economy, and in trying to understand how Purpose Economy organizations like Etsy, Interface, and Airbnb differ from their predecessors of even a decade earlier.

As I began to study the pioneers of the Purpose Economy, it became clear that marketing, human resources, and strategic planning were giving way to new methods of organizing and working, and that in order to thrive, organizations would need to rethink the ways they were operating in this new economy.

And those are just the impacts of the Purpose Economy within organizations. We will likely also see radical changes to everything from government to parenting to health care.

There are unprecedented opportunities that exist in this nascent economy. It is ours to design and own, to create and expand markets in still unimaginable ways. As current and future leaders, we have the opportunity to improve the lives of billions of people.

The Purpose Economy 2.0

In the early spring of 2013, I sat down and drafted *The Purpose Economy*. I shared my insights and stories from the front lines to help inspire and enable everyone to embrace, build, and own the new economy. The book was set to be published in September of the same year, but after a 15-minute conversation with Eric Ries, author of *The Lean Startup*, we switched gears and decided to treat the manuscript as a beta version and not as the finished book. We printed 2,000 copies and sent them to pioneers and thought leaders in the new economy. We asked them to contribute their ideas and observations about the Purpose Economy, the book, and the concept. We asked them to share their Post-it notes. I wrote the book you are now reading, but in many ways it was co-authored by the numerous people who shared their stories and ideas.

Armed with the generous and insightful feedback from so many thinking partners from around the world, I created a final set of Post-it notes, which became the structure for this book. *The Purpose Economy* is not meant to be read as a treatise, but as a work in progress and a call to action for all of us working towards building an economy that serves people and the planet.

In this book, you will explore the evolution of markets within the Purpose Economy and the key levers that can be used to advance them, as well as the new approaches to running an organization across sectors that can thrive in this new era. But the most important section in this book is the one about you. At the core of the Purpose Economy is people's need and desire to find their own professional purpose. This felt like an impossible task when I founded Taproot, but just over a decade later, the key ingredients have become clear and have been proven powerful.

This book presents an opportunity of unprecedented potential: an economy that will not only continue to generate jobs and resources, but one that also has the capability to improve the lives of billions of people. But much of this potential lies in how we as leaders move forward and how we frame and invest in this new economy. It is, at its core, the first economy built for humans.

So grab some Post-it notes, and let's get started.

SECTION ONE

WELCOME TO THE PURPOSE ECONOMY

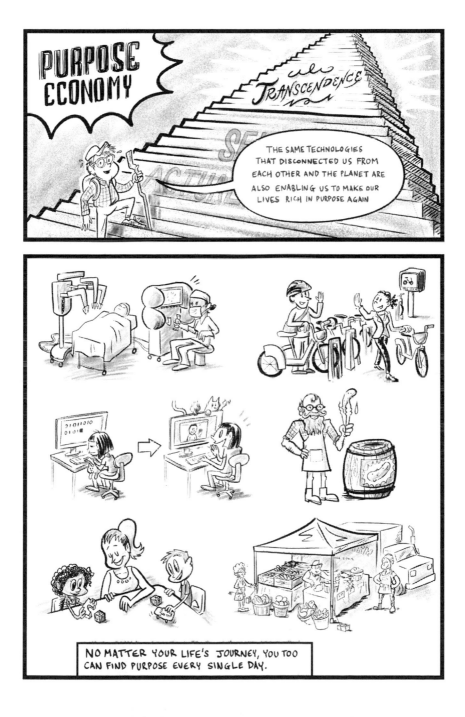

I

The Purpose Economy

Every weekday morning at 8:00, the Taproot Foundation database emails me a report of the names, professions, and locations of everyone who had applied to join our team of pro bono consultants in the previous 24 hours. Usually dozens of names long, the report also includes a short essay explaining why the applicant wanted to donate a hundred hours of their time to one of our nonprofit partners. In the dozen years since I founded Taproot, I have likely read 25 thousand of these responses, and while each of them are unique, the motivations remain remarkably consistent:

> "I'll be honest—my current 9 to 5 copywriting job is not inspiring, and it's not making the world a better place."

> "I love to contribute my professional skills to any worthwhile cause.... Money can't buy the sense of fulfillment one feels knowing that you have invested in the hopes and dreams of others through organizations such as Taproot."

> "My passion for helping people is rivaled only by my passion for automating things with computers. I want to combine these two things."

> "I find pro bono work so much more rewarding than a paycheck job. It really helps take my skills and talent to

their full potential and get the most of them. It's a personal opportunity to explore and stretch my creative/marketing abilities."

"I feel blessed to have been able to go to school and succeed in my career, and feel compelled to use the skills afforded by the opportunities I've been given to help deserving organizations that can use the help."

In just over twelve years, these professionals have enabled Taproot to donate over $100 million in pro bono services—an average of $8,000 per volunteer—making us the largest nonprofit consulting firm in the in the United States. Their payment? Purpose.

When I say purpose, I mean more than serving others and the planet. Service is certainly at the core, but in speaking with hundreds of professionals and reading thousands of essays, I've discovered that there are two other key sources of purpose people seek: a sense of community and the opportunity for self-expression and personal growth. In other words, they pursue personal, social, and societal purpose.

An extraordinarily powerful force drives the desire to tap into these rich sources of meaning in our lives. Since launching Taproot in 2001, I have witnessed that force not only change the lives of thousands of professionals, but also begin to drive a remarkable shift in our economy. This shift has given rise to whole new breeds of organizations, products, relationships, and services that discover innovative approaches to prioritize purpose in people's lives, while often addressing the most intractable social and environmental problems.

This shift is so substantial and pervasive that I now believe we are in the early days of the emergence of a "Purpose Economy"— the fourth American economy in our history. While the Purpose

Economy certainly does not dominate our gross domestic product, it is growing quickly. Furthermore, as I will argue in this book, it is likely that in 20 years, the pursuit of purpose will eclipse the third American economy, the Information Economy.

Purpose, Purpose—Everywhere

I'm not an economist, a sociologist, or a psychologist. I am an entrepreneur. Entrepreneurs constantly look for opportunities, hoping to find emerging trends or spot inspiration for new products or services. This kind of pattern recognition first helped me see the enormous potential for pro bono and has now helped me discern the underlying thread in what appears to be myriad emerging trends of the last decade. It's helped me comprehend how they are all driven by the pursuit of purpose—together, they create the Purpose Economy.

For more than a decade, I focused intensely on achieving the Taproot Foundation's mission. When I finally came up for air and reflected on our progress, I realized that the pro bono movement was nearing a tipping point, as pro bono service had started to go mainstream. But I also realized that our success was part of a much larger movement. The public was changing their priorities, and new organizations, products, relationships and services that were once niche were now finding markets.

These powerful shifts in public desire are changing what we buy, how we buy it, from whom we buy it, why we buy it, and how much of it we buy. We are sharing everything, from bikes and cars to extra rooms in our homes. We can once again buy and sell handcrafted products with ease. Grocery stores now sell more local and organic food, and farmers' markets have popped up all over the country.

In the last ten years, social innovation has become big business. Conferences and magazines are dedicated to the topic, and legions of consultants and entrepreneurs help individuals and companies adapt to this new way of operating. Under President Obama, the White House now has an Office of Social Innovation and Civic Participation.

Open almost any newspaper or magazine or look at a list of bestsellers, and you'll find evidence of this change in priorities. A whole new genre of "solution journalism" has emerged, with media outlets like the Solutions Journalism Network and GOOD covering social impact solutions, as well as established publications, from *Fast Company* to Germany's *Capital* shifting their focus from business to an expanded focus on business and society. Even *The Economist* entered the game with the publication of Matthew Bishop's *Philanthrocapitalism: How the Rich Can Save the World*.

Harvard professor and corporate strategist Michael Porter launched the "Social Progress Imperative," a global index that strives to look beyond gross domestic product and provides a ranking of countries globally, based on the extent to which they are meeting the social and environmental needs of their citizens. It is one of several similar efforts, including the United Nations' Universal Periodic Review, that focuses on aspects such as human rights and social impact rather than economic factors in order to evaluate nations' progress.

The conversation about work is also rapidly evolving, with the emergence of new fields of research (such as positive psychology) and new search and recruiting firms focused solely on helping people find meaningful work. Search firms like ReWork, On-Ramps, Idealist, and Commongood Careers (which uses the catchy tagline, "Will work for social change") are thriving. Books like Adam Grant's *Give and Take* and Martin Seligman's *Flourish* are redefining not just what drives employee engagement and productivity, but what improves employee well-being. These new concepts inspire different approaches to management and careers. Applications from the best talent in the nation have flooded these firms, just as Teach for America has been now for over a decade.

A generation of Purpose Economy pioneers, like Whole Foods Market's John Mackey and Virgin's Richard Branson, are challenging others to follow their lead and to create new frameworks both to do well and to do good, which raises the bar for the business community and turns successful theories into movements. Richard Branson launched the B Team, a coalition aiming to go beyond traditional corporate social responsibility, and instead embrace what they call Plan B: "a plan that puts people and the planet alongside profit." John Mackey and his team are promoting a new model for business he calls Conscious Capitalism, which inspired his book of the same name.

Other large corporations have shown signs of new, purpose-focused frameworks as well. Some of the most traditional companies like Deloitte and Pepsi have started to put their toes in the water, as their leaders recognize that while they can't change overnight, they can develop long-term visions to make purpose a priority. In light of this, they have taken proactive and prudent steps in that direction. Pepsi's CEO Indra Nooyi has framed their north star as "performance with purpose" and begun to make "healthy eats" and the environment core to their success. Deloitte, a consultancy with 200,000 employees around the globe, has made it a priority to embrace a culture of purpose, realizing that successful companies must be "keenly aware of the purpose they fulfill for clients, employees, community, and other groups," and they have integrated those goals into their business's core activities.

Even Morgan Stanley recently got into the game with its announcement of the multi-billion-dollar Institute for Sustainable Investing. Finance is slowly changing to thrive in the new economy. Several states are experimenting with social impact bonds, and others are experimenting with new governance structures to address the financing needs of organizations that don't neatly fit into commercial or nonprofit categories.

Much like technology a few decades ago, purpose has now become a business imperative. In today's world, running an organization without an intentional emphasis on purpose for employees and customers is like running an organization in the early 1990s and failing to implement technology.

Little of this is truly new, of course. Farmers' markets existed long before chain stores. Social impact bonds appeared in Israel in the midcentury. During the 1960s in the United States and Europe, there existed several large-scale experiments with communal ownership. *Mother Jones* magazine has reported on social problems and impact for decades. But what we are seeing now is the acceleration and the commercialization of those activities, fueled by new forms of capital, that allow these developments to move from the fringe to the mainstream. We are approaching the tipping point, where the Purpose Economy has matured enough to move from the fringes of society to the heart of the U.S. economy and, increasingly, to those around the globe.

What Is the Purpose Economy?

The Purpose Economy describes the new context and set of ways in which people and organizations are focused on creating value, and it defines the organizing principle for innovation and growth. Each of the three previous economies were unique to the context and set of conditions of the day, all of which served as forces to impact the markets in each economy. The Purpose Economy is defined by the quest for people to have more purpose in their lives. It is an economy where value lies in establishing purpose for employees and customers—through serving needs greater than their own, enabling personal growth, and building community.

The emergence of purpose as the new organizing principle in our economy is a product of our current moment in time. It is based on where we stand in history today: our current culture, values, education, technological abilities, social organizations, political realities, and the state of our natural environment. Each part of our world has gone through a radical transformation in the last few decades, and they are now converging into a new set of processes to change the way society operates.

We can see these changes in many ways through little things in our everyday lives, such as the food we're eating and where we're shopping. They affect how we live and how we work, and they are empowering people to have rich and fulfilling careers by creating meaningful value for themselves and others.

These changes in today's society have created the Purpose Economy, which is the umbrella over many movements and pursuits of meaning. Many writers and researchers have discovered new theories to explain this shift in culture, such as the striving for community, the need for self-expression, or the longing for happiness. The Purpose Economy explains where markets meet movements, as individuals step out to create their own means of finding purpose through their work.

Three Types of Purpose

To understand the Purpose Economy, it is critical to understand purpose and how it is created for people. The definition and nature of purpose is often misunderstood. There are three well-researched, core categories that consistently echo through the words of the professionals who applied to the Taproot Foundation: personal purpose, social purpose, and societal purpose. Together, they represent the needs that the new Purpose Economy addresses.

Warren Brown, Kristine Ashe, and Kate Atwood each came to points in their careers when they decided they needed to make a change to increase purpose in their lives. They each created new organizations to realize this need, but each was driven by a need for a different kind of purpose. Their following stories help to illustrate the three types of purpose that are transforming the economy.

I. Personal Purpose

Warren Brown was one of over a million lawyers in the United States. As he describes, "My moment of truth came very late on a Friday night when I was still practicing law. On this night, I was

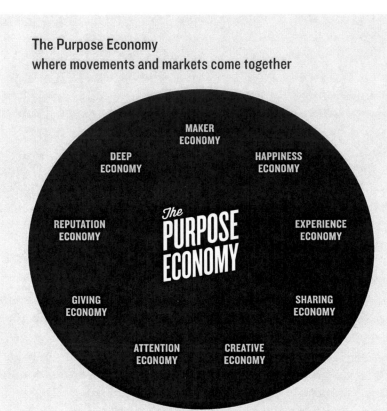

The Purpose Economy
where movements and markets come together

MAKER
ECONOMY

DEEP
ECONOMY

HAPPINESS
ECONOMY

REPUTATION
ECONOMY

The PURPOSE ECONOMY

EXPERIENCE
ECONOMY

GIVING
ECONOMY

SHARING
ECONOMY

ATTENTION
ECONOMY

CREATIVE
ECONOMY

The Purpose Economy helps explain many of the movements that have gained traction in the last decade, including resource sharing, maker (e.g. do-it-yourself), happiness, reputation, giving, creative and experience. Together, these movements are the heart of the macroeconomic evolution that points to purpose as the new driver of the American economy.

making a cake for one of the senior managers in my office, and I was trying to make it look extra nice." He was good at his job, but it was only a job—what he really loved was baking with and for his friends. What started as a hobby became a bakery, CakeLove, and later a café, the LoveCafe. Both the bakery and café became wildly successful, and he eventually left his job as an attorney. And yet, just a few years in, Warren wasn't happy. Despite doing what he loved, he was in fact spending all of his time running the bakery. What he loved most was talking to his customers about cake and creating the kinds of amazing cakes that wowed them. As it turned out, his passion had been making cakes, not managing a bakery.

After recognizing the gap between what he was doing and what he wanted to be doing, Warren hired a manager to run his business and refocused his energy on baking and looking for new ways to create cakes. He talked to his customers about what they loved and found that while his customers clearly loved cake, they had trouble eating it neatly. After a little trial and error, a solution emerged: Cake Bites, small cakes baked and served in tiny jars. The Cake Bites were an instant hit, and Warren was soon selling them to Whole Foods. His business boomed. By following his passion, Warren had not only found a profound sense of purpose but built a great business in the process. "In living my passion, when I wake up, I'm all go. I'm spiritually amped—ready and willing to dive into the satisfaction I get every day from baking." Passion is a crucial element of purpose.

For Warren, the pursuit of purpose was deeply personal. It began with him recognizing a problem, cultivating the self-awareness to understand what needed to change, and pushing himself to make the necessary changes so that he could grow. It's no different for our generation. We find purpose when we are do things we love, attempt new challenges, and express our voice to the world.

There's no better example of personal purpose than the remarkable success of Etsy, a marketplace where over a million artists and makers sell their wares. In just five short years, Etsy has enabled thousands of professionals to quit their day jobs for work that is meaningful for them. The company reports that there are now more Etsy sellers in New York City than taxi drivers. By creating demand for handmade goods, from jewelry to art to furniture, Etsy has made it commercially viable for people to do the work that enabled their self-expression and growth as craftspeople.

2. Social Purpose

Kristine Ashe's family was fractured and living all over the country. She longed to share her life with them but knew it was unlikely unless she created the opportunity for it to happen. Though she knew very little about farming or winemaking, Kristine decided to buy a vineyard.

Unlike Warren Brown and his connection to the craft of baking, Kristine's dream was not to make wine, but rather to create a business that would bring her family together and build a community. The wine business had a relatively low barrier to entry and strong community of mentorship in winemaking—you looked to your neighbors for help. Her hope was that it would be a way for to finally bring her family together in one place, all working on the vineyard. It could be a business that was focused on community and relationships.

Remarkably, her field of dreams worked. Kristine built the vineyard around her family, creating a ranch that allowed her to work with her kids by her side. Her extended family also got involved in ways she never imagined. Her sister moved to the farm, and her brother-in-law now leads the vineyard's operations. Her father even built their website.

Kristine decided to call the vineyard Entre Nous, French for "between us". Kristine explained her motivation to create the vineyard: "The connections between us bring the greatest joy, the highest passion, and the most authentic satisfaction in our frequently impassive, impersonal, and impatient world." The work of winemaking was rewarding and pushed her to her limits, but it was the ability to share that work with the people she loved that made it truly meaningful and gave her such a strong sense of purpose.

Research shows that purpose is not a solo act. Michael Steger at Colorado State University has created a Laboratory for the Study of Meaning and Quality of Life. In his study of over 250,000 people, he found evidence that what Kristine had felt applies on a much broader level. When it comes to meaning in life, relationships matter to humans more than anything else. They reinforce our sense of value, require us to engage, and ultimately help us grow.[1]

> We often find purpose through social interaction. This constitutes much of the success of Facebook and other social media sites like Tumblr and YouTube. They have made a business of creating a platform for people to express themselves to others in their network and beyond. While social media isn't as rich in purpose as true communion in person with friends, it still enables us to share our journey with others, which amplifies the purpose in our lives. Social media, then, combines personal purpose and social purpose—perhaps the reason for its ever-increasing popularity.

3. Societal Purpose

When NASCAR's Kate Atwood was asked to speak at a camp for kids who had lost a parent, she wasn't expecting her life and career trajectory to change. But when she found herself in front of hundreds of kids telling the story of losing her own mother to cancer when she was twelve years old, something shifted. It was the first time she had ever shared her story. "Until that day, the death of my mom had been about me," Kate shared with me. "After that day, I knew it was much bigger than myself."

Later that evening, a little girl about ten years old tapped Kate on her shoulder and asked, "Are you Kate?" "Yes," she replied. The girl then continued to tell her the story of losing her own mom and dad in a car accident. "To this day, that moment stands as the time I first brushed up with the power of purpose," she explains.

"Two years later, at the tender age of 22, this thirst [to find purpose in my life] led me to my boss's office, to let her know I was leaving the company to start a nonprofit for kids who had lost a parent or sibling." Kate left NASCAR to start Kate's Club. For the next ten years, she expanded it, and it became a well-established community for children and teens in Atlanta navigating life after the death of a parent or sibling. It was with Kate's Club that her personality manifested, both as a survivor of loss and as a kid who just wanted to know that grief changed her life but did not end it. She learned that your darkest moment can become your biggest gift, if you are able to make it about something beyond yourself.

The most powerful source of purpose comes from this concept: purpose comes when we know we have done something that we believe matters—to others, to society, and to ourselves. From the small and mundane daily choices we make to systemic and historic impact, we strive to contribute to the well-being of the world around us. Societal purpose isn't isolated to volunteering and philanthropy, or careers in education and social work. While these often spark feelings of purpose, we can also derive purpose through decisions about how we consume, from decreasing our carbon footprint to buying local produce at the farmers' market. We can also discover meaning through our daily work, where we help the people on our teams and provide consumers with our products and services.

Seventh Generation makes cleaning, baby and feminine personal care products that aim to be healthy and safe for the air,
the surfaces, the fabrics, the pets, and the people within the
home—and for the community and environment outside it.
Founded in 1988, Seventh Generation was one of the first successful companies to build a brand around creating products
and services that help consumers better care for the earth. Investing in environmental sustainability is one of the most powerful (and literal) ways to do something bigger than yourself. By
making these products available for the mass market, Seventh
Generation enables people caring for their homes and families
to make purpose part of their daily routine.

At its foundation, the Purpose Economy creates purpose for
people. It serves the critical need for people to develop themselves, be
part of a community, and affect something greater than themselves.
It may sound utopian, but there is evidence in almost every industry
and throughout our culture that this shift is already underway. The
Information Economy, which has driven innovation and economic
growth for approximately the past fifty years, is only the most
recent evolutionary leap in the history of the global economy. We
are now in the process of making the next big leap.

2
Economic Evolution

Every once in a while, someone writes a Ph.D. dissertation that is not only read by others, but also radically impacts that field of study. One such dissertation was written by my uncle, Marc Porat, while studying economics at Stanford in 1977. In his nine-volume dissertation, *The Information Economy: Definition and Measurement,* he coined the term "Information Economy," arguing that a great transition to an information-based economy had been underway since the middle of the century.[1] He connected the dots to see the rise of the third economy in our history. Now, the conditions and tools created by the Information Economy are aiding in the emergence of the Purpose Economy.

This is the emergent nature of economic evolution: each new, dominant economy grows out of the foundation of the prior dominant economy, though the new one doesn't entirely displace its predecessor. Rather, it complements and builds from it, tackling problems and serving human needs in new and distinctive ways.

Marc's richly detailed thesis can be summarized this way: We were once an agrarian society of farmers and dealt in wheat and corn. We then became an industrial society, working in factories and producing cars and airplanes. As of the mid- to late 20th century, we had become an information society, with nearly half of our economy based on transforming, transferring, and using information. 20 years after my uncle made his argument, the Information Economy would be credited with comprising 63 percent of the United States' GDP.[2]

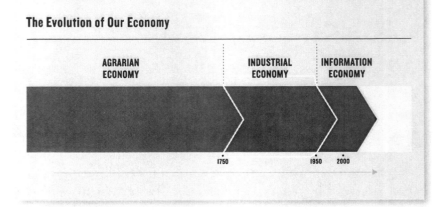

The Evolution of Our Economy

AGRARIAN ECONOMY | INDUSTRIAL ECONOMY | INFORMATION ECONOMY

1750   1950   2000

Before the Information Economy

Marc's theory was really the next chapter of a much longer economic evolution that spans more than a million years, beginning with the very first stone tool. Since the beginning of human history, we have developed countless ways of improving our quality of life and extending our lifespan. But about twelve thousand years ago, there was a major evolutionary leap forward. We began the transition from nomadic hunters and gatherers to farmers, cultivating land to provide more stable sources of food. We thus became agrarian, centering our prosperity and culture around our agricultural interests. As we learned to farm, we built better tools and established the early science of agriculture. And as the farms grew, so did the first villages and towns. This period also marked the beginning of land ownership, social classes, and slavery. Wealth and freedom were tied to owning land and the ability to optimize its output.

The next major economic evolution, also tied to optimizing output, occurred more quickly. In 1712, British inventor Thomas Newcomen created the commercial steam engine in England. It was first used as a water pump and—despite its inefficiencies—was able to generate the power of twenty horses walking in a circle, a groundbreaking feat for that time. But even more impressive were the monumental gains in life expectancy that followed this first industrial boom. In 1796, the average person only lived to be 24, but just a hundred years later, that same person could live to be 48.

The new forms of transportation, communication, and mechanized goods invented during and since the Industrial Revolution have made life much more comfortable in many parts of the world. They have also created whole new classes of people and occupations. Many industries needed more and more specialized labor and saw education expand to develop the talent needed, and as people moved from farms to factories, vocational services were introduced, which supported migrants and youth in finding work. Men developed modern democracy. International trade boomed, connecting cultures around the world. As humans, our mental abilities were enabling us to make biological evolution de facto irrelevant—we had taken control of the process and produced unbelievable results. Of course, all this came at a great cost to the natural world, with pollution and the mass extinction of countless species.

Too much and too long, we seem to have surrendered community excellence and community values in the mere accumulation of material things. Our gross national product...if we should judge America by that—counts air pollution and cigarette advertising, and ambulances to clear our highways of carnage. It counts special locks for our doors and the jails for those who break them. It counts the destruction of our redwoods and the loss of our natural wonder in chaotic sprawl. It counts napalm and the cost of a nuclear warhead, and armored cars for police who fight riots in our streets. It counts Whitman's rifle and Speck's knife, and the television programs which glorify violence in order to sell toys to our children.

Yet the gross national product does not allow for the health of our children, the quality of their education, or the joy of their play. It does not include the beauty of our poetry or the strength of our marriages; the intelligence of our public debate or the integrity of our public officials. It measures neither our wit nor our courage; neither our wisdom nor our learning; neither our compassion nor our devotion to our country; it measures everything, in short, except that which makes life worthwhile. And it tells us everything about America except why we are proud that we are Americans.

—Robert F. Kennedy, 1968

The Information Economy

At the start of the 20th century, the name of the game was efficiency and output, which launched an obsession with building faster and more efficient means of production. By the middle of the 20th century, the marketplace was dominated by large corporations and institutions, which created a new kind of workplace built on hierarchy and development within an organization. Labor became increasingly segmented into narrow functional roles, and new vocational training and professional schools were created to respond to the need for more focused training within one specialization. The bigger the organizations grew and the more specialized they became, the greater their need for improved communication and information systems. Society needed better and more reliable information to engineer our lives and work.

At the turn of the last century, Braun and Marconi developed wireless telegraphy, which began the transition into the Information Economy. The telegraph would eventually be followed by the calculator, television, computer, and the Internet. We were now in the business of information, and it was the ability to create and manipulate information that ruled the day. The human race had done it again, but this time, we had actually used our minds, rather than our physical abilities, to increase our mental capacity. That is, we had developed ways to externalize and accelerate our mental functions.

With the advent of modern technology, the workforce has begun to change again. We no longer have a single lifetime employer that takes us under its wing for our entire career. The tenure in a given company has dropped precipitously, with the average employee staying at a job for a mere four and a half years.[3] Work has become unstable, decreasingly tied to organizational structures, and the market for labor is now global and increasingly virtual. In some ways, we are becoming de facto freelancers, on our own and navigating great uncertainty in every direction.

We have created new idols. The worship of the ancient golden calf...has returned in a new and ruthless guise in the idolatry of money and the dictatorship of an impersonal economy lacking a truly human purpose.

In our time humanity, is experiencing a turning-point in its history, as we can see from the advances being made in so many fields. We can only praise the steps being taken to improve people's welfare in areas such as health care, education and communications. At the same time we have to remember that the majority of our contemporaries are barely living from

> day to day, with dire consequences. A number of diseases are spreading. The hearts of many people are gripped by fear and desperation, even in the so-called rich countries.
>
> The joy of living frequently fades, lack of respect for others and violence are on the rise, and inequality is increasingly evident. It is a struggle to live and, often, to live with precious little dignity. This epochal change has been set in motion by the enormous qualitative, quantitative, rapid and cumulative advances occurring in the sciences and in technology, and by their instant application in different areas of nature and of life. We are in an age of knowledge and information, which has led to new and often anonymous kinds of power.
>
> —Pope Francis, 2013

After the Information Economy

The instability caused by these major structural changes and magnified by the economic recession brought with it a need to find stability and a future path within ourselves, rather than from an employer. This shift has placed meaning and purpose at the heart of the contemporary workforce—purpose, rather than career longevity, now provides the stability we need. As workplace researchers Paul Hartung and Brian Taber describe, "Rather than fitting self to jobs and readying self to develop a career, workers now must focus increasingly on constructing self in work rather than advancing self in an organization."[4]

This shift cascades beyond work. The broader instability, combined with globalization and other unsettling changes (including our climate), has prompted us to prioritize purpose in other aspects of our lives as well. It has inspired fundamentalism around the world as people seek new organizations and clear answers to help anchor their lives. And it has inspired the purpose generation, Millennials, who are increasingly constructing their identities around purpose to make sense of the rapidly evolving world and their equally fluctuating role in it.

And yet, this is not an economic or social evolution; it is how we manipulate the world to better serve our needs. Each new economy evolves out of a distinctive set of conditions and is characterized by an innate set of products and means of production. Just as the farmers of the Agrarian Economy made use of the earth to grow crops and raise livestock, the industrialists extracted raw materials for producing energy and fueling a new breed of powerful machines. The expertise developed in building increasingly sophisticated machines was key to the rise of the Information Economy. And though the computer was conceived by a mathematician, Alan Turing, it was built and commercialized by engineers. Engineers also pioneered the series of new technologies that formed the infrastructure of the Information Economy, culminating with the introduction of the Internet.

Of course, information, as well as the need to disperse and manage it, wasn't new either: the Information Economy has been around since the first teacher. What was remarkable in 1977, when my uncle wrote his thesis, was the magnitude of its growth and the speed at which it was gaining dominance in the overall economy. This same transition is now happening with the Purpose Economy. Its evolution is gaining speed, and it is becoming a driver in large segments of the overall economy.

The notion that the Purpose Economy is rapidly eclipsing the Information Economy may seem premature—after all, we just recently entered the new era of "the cloud" and mobile computing. But this is also in line with the history of economic evolution. Not only is the economy always evolving, but the pace of that evolution quickens with each transition. While the Agrarian Economy emerged over the course of some 8,000 years, the Industrial Economy required less than 150 years to diminish the percentage of agrarian workers from 90 percent to 2 percent.

The Information Economy emerged in earnest in the 1950s and is unlikely to last as the dominant economy for another hundred years. Signs of its waning have already surfaced. Pioneer venture capitalist William Draper III recently shared with me that over the last ten years, the returns on new Information Economy ventures haven't been as strong as they had been in the decades before, because most of the new ventures are what he calls "me too" kinds of efforts. The pitches coming into most venture capitalist offices now aren't for new, groundbreaking ideas, but rather ideas for incremental improvements or niche versions of successful existing technology platforms, like social media, cloud services, e-commerce, "big data," and gaming.

At first glance, many of the hot new companies today, like local retail market maker Zaarly, look like Information Economy companies, but they are at their core part of this new economy. As I explore in Section Three, their DNA is different.

A common refrain we hear from technologists and the media is that the Information Economy is just getting started. Silicon Valley and Silicon Alley are home to some of the world's most successful companies, many of them start-ups. But I'm not suggesting that its evolution will stop, or that it won't still be a major driving force in overall economic development. I'm suggesting that in terms of setting the course, the Purpose Economy will eventually edge it out. In fact, I believe the Purpose Economy—like the once-emerging Information Economy—already accounts for a much larger portion of the overall economy than may be readily apparent.

Sizing the Purpose Economy

When I first learned of my uncle Marc's work on the Information

Economy, I assumed that the set of industries and professions officially designated as the information sector had grown to be larger than those in the manufacturing sector. But even 30 years later, this isn't the case. In 2009, the U.S. Census GDP tables showed the information industry at a meager 5 percent of the economy, compared to manufacturing at 11 percent.[5] What Marc argued was more nuanced. While in the official GDP tables, the information industry was made up only of publishing, software, motion pictures, recording, broadcasting, telecommunications, and information and data processing services (this holds true today as well), he saw that a much wider range of functions, products, and services in the economy were driven by the creation, analysis, or management of information, from education to risk management, to even the postal service.

Marc proposed that we needed to broaden the definition of the information industries to also include these sectors and functions:

- knowledge production and invention (private R&D and information services)
- information distribution and communication (education, public information, services, telecommunications)
- risk management (insurance and finance industries)
- search and coordination (brokerage industries, advertising)
- information processing and transmission services (computer based information processing, telecommunications infrastructure)
- information goods (calculators, semiconductors, computers)
- selected government activities (education and postal service)
- support facilities (buildings, office furniture)
- wholesale and retail trade in information goods and services

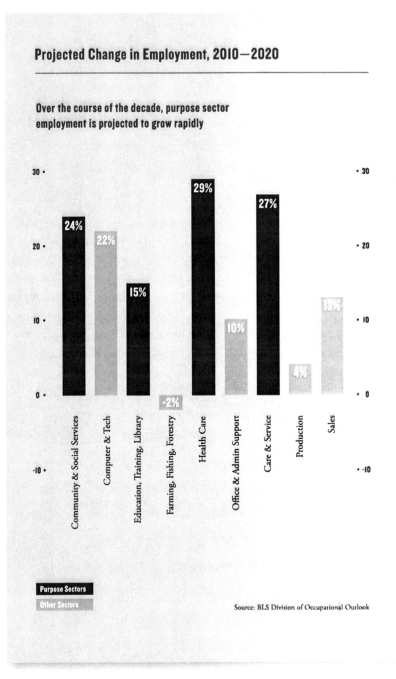

Projected Change in Employment, 2010—2020

Over the course of the decade, purpose sector employment is projected to grow rapidly

- Community & Social Services: 24%
- Computer & Tech: 22%
- Education, Training, Library: 15%
- Farming, Fishing, Forestry: -2%
- Health Care: 29%
- Office & Admin Support: 10%
- Care & Service: 27%
- Production: 4%
- Sales: 13%

Purpose Sectors
Other Sectors

Source: BLS Division of Occupational Outlook

We must analyze the Purpose Economy similarly. It might seem to be mostly comprised of the nonprofit sector, but much more should be included. If we just look just at the nonprofit sector, it's interesting to note that it is similar in size to the more traditional definition of the information sector. In 2011, it stood at 5.4 percent of the GDP. That represented a 25 percent increase over a similar measure ten years earlier, but one certainly couldn't describe it as a dominant part of our economy.[5] But defining the Purpose Economy solely in terms of the nonprofit sector is like describing the Information Economy solely in terms of the activity in Silicon Valley today. It excludes a big part of the picture that lies outside of this central sector. The impact of both economies reaches far beyond GDP statistics, but the Purpose Economy transcends facts and figures to grasp at something even deeper—the aspirations of the human soul.

The nonprofit sector is certainly core to the Purpose Economy, but it is by no means the only sector driven by the provision of services to improve lives, inspire personal growth, or expand community. The Purpose Economy impacts all the sectors in the broader economy, like the Information Economy has done and continues to do.

These outputs are part of many industries, some of which overlap those Marc included in the Information Economy; for example, education accounts for $1.3 trillion of our GDP.[7] Education, after all, is one of the richest elements of the Purpose Economy, but it is also deeply connected to how we transfer information in our society. The health care industry, which contributes 18 percent of our GDP, should also be included, as well as research that improves our lives—like cancer research, the development of genomics, solar energy, and new sustainable materials. We also need to include models that support expression and community building: companies like Facebook and YouTube, which produce some of the $20 billion dollars in annual revenue from the social media sector.[8]

Government programs also belong under the rubric of the Purpose Economy, especially in other parts of the world, where the portion of government that is dedicated to purpose-based missions is quite substantial. In my work outside the United States, I've discovered that every nation has different definitions for sectors and industries. The nonprofit sector as we know it in the United States doesn't really exist in the vast majority of countries. In nations like Denmark and England, many of the functions of the American nonprofit sector are run by government agencies or commercial entities.

For this reason, the United Nations and other global organizations have struggled to find ways to create linkages between countries when the sectors don't line up neatly. To help support those linkages, the United Nations' Civil Society team had to find a definition of activities, rather than a particular sector, that would enable cross-border comparisons. They ended up dividing civil society organizations into two groups by type of activity: service-oriented and expressive. Service-oriented activities include housing, social services, education, and health care. They defined expressive activities as advocacy, arts and culture, sports and recreation, and interest representation. These activities, regardless of which sector or industry they fall into, constitute part of the Purpose Economy.

And there are many other pockets of Purpose Economy growth. The market for lifestyle of health and sustainability (LOHAS) has doubled to $600 billion in five years, covering products and services focused on health and fitness, the environment, personal development, sustainable living, and social justice. The peer-to-peer or sharing market is now estimated at $26 billion.[9]

This new market includes everything from sharing bikes to cars to housing. More than 500 cities across 49 countries now have bike sharing programs with a combined fleet of over 500,000 bicycles.[10] And new online markets like Etsy and Zaarly have just started to scratch the surface of maker and local markets. In 2013, Etsy surpassed $1 billion in sales, and farmers' markets now make up the fastest growing part of our food sector, doubling in the last decade.[11]

Sustainability is a major market in the new economy. Investing in the health and well-being of future generations is an act of serving something greater than ourselves. In many cases, it still requires us to give up short-term benefits in order to help others in the long term.

Green building is booming. Green building materials generate $116 billion globally, and that number is expected to more than double by the end of the decade. Opportunities particularly abound in nonresidential construction—by 2015, this sector will compromise half the construction market, amounting to $120 billion.[12] The drive for sustainability is also leading the energy market, with wind, solar, geothermal, hydropower, biomass, and biofuels representing one-third of all new power capacity additions as of 2011.[13]

One area that is remarkably lagging, however, is education. There has been significant investment in education over the last dozen years as many of the brightest minds in the nation, from Bill Gates to Eli Broad, have tried to crack the code on student success. We have seen an explosion in charter schools, technology in the classroom, organic school lunches, and dozens of other experiments. Some have shown hints of potential, but it is clear to most innovators in the field that a revolutionary innovation, more than an evolutionary one, is needed. Today, the United States doesn't even rank in the top thirty nations in educational status, and our health care outcomes are sadly worse. Though many sectors have flourished in the Purpose Economy, others have fallen further behind.

The portion of the economy connected to purpose will continue to grow as companies dedicate more of their business to creating purpose, and as more innovative organizations, such as hybrid non- and for-profit companies, are created. That was true also for the Information Economy. Leaders of that economy, like HP and IBM, started with a foot still in manufacturing, creating hardware to store and manage information. Today, we see the early Purpose Economy stars anchored in Information Economy platforms; Facebook, which enables self-expression and community on a massive scale, is a great example. Kickstarter, which now provides more funding for the arts than the National Endowment for the Arts, is another.

With the rise of the Information Economy, most companies eventually adopted information-driven systems and tools into their operations and products, such as GPS in cars and robotics in manufacturing. It wasn't until the auto industry in Detroit really embraced the Information Economy that they were able to turn their fortunes around. But even though these companies adopted the practices, they won't ever be an Oracle or Microsoft, core Information Economy companies.

Many companies will survive and even thrive without embracing purpose, but it will only become more difficult as the labor market shifts and consumer priorities evolve. Most companies and organizations will not be pure Purpose Economy companies like Etsy, but they will change their practices radically, as they did with the last evolution. In the nations of the developed world, most people's basic needs for sustenance, shelter, and information are met. Accordingly, we have emerged from the Agrarian, Industrial and Information economies to the Purpose Economy, that we might fulfill our higher-order needs: meaning and purpose. Meeting these needs will not only enrich our own lives, but the lives of everyone around the planet.

3
The Ten Drivers of the New Economy

As with each economy before it, the Purpose Economy naturally progresses from the previous economy. The Purpose Economy is only possible because of the Information Economy, not only because of the amazing capabilities that economy created, but also the positive and negative externalities it generated. We also still see many antecedents of the new economy in the Industrial Economy, which is less than a hundred years behind us, as the core of our society. But ultimately, there were a special set of circumstances and key drivers that gave rise to the Purpose Economy and that continue to contribute to its growth.

I. Human-Scale Technology

Technology has evolved over the last ten years, from enabling us to move online to now enabling us to find purpose online.

When I began working in Silicon Valley in the 1990s, people had just begun to realize the possibilities of how to commercialize the Internet. Most start-ups simply focused on how to move online, build a brand, and claim market share. How to capitalize on that market share was an issue for the future. Companies took an existing business or market and found ways that it could operate online with greater efficiency; the innovation was simply taking what was offline and putting it online.

In a publication from the fall of 2013, Reid Hoffman, founder of LinkedIn, does a great job of summarizing this first phase of the web. He explains that the first websites enabled people to search and transact via flat directories. For example, the *Philadelphia*

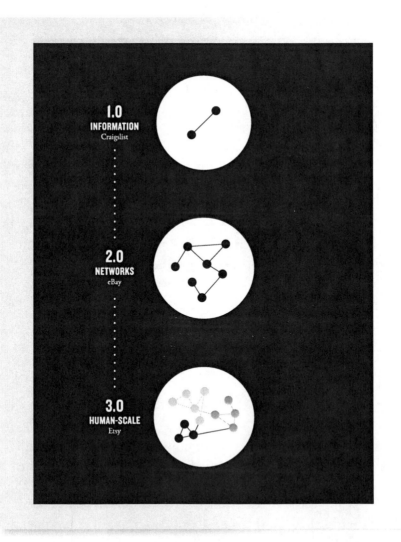

Inquirer put its existing classifieds online to make them searchable. Citi enabled their customers to make payments online. Websites revolved around providing information to their users.

Then came the second phase of the Internet, where the networks of users became a core part of the developed solutions. Users could now search and transact via networks. Rather than search the *Philadelphia Inquirer*'s classifieds, we could use eBay, which implemented a seller's reputation into the search for goods and the resulting purchase. Rather than just make payments online at Citi, we used PayPal, which was able to create network transactions between users. LinkedIn, then, was part of this second wave, as it evolved past sites like Monster.com to allow us to assess professionals through a network of relationships between users.

Google, too, was built on this 2.0 Internet, moving beyond searching web pages to allow us to search the network of links between users. Letters became emails (online letters), and emails became tweets (networked letters). Meetings became online discussion forums and eventually crowdsourcing.

Social media is at the heart of Internet 2.0. By helping move people from consumers to creators online, social media drove the web's next generation to emerge. It sparked our collective imagination in thinking about how technology could be leveraged for self-expression, community building, and service. And as our lives become more public, we are increasingly conscious of "personal brands." So many people now have windows into our activities, network, and points of view, and this new level of transparency has created new ways to display our aspirational selves. A large part of that display is the demonstration that we are rich in purpose. We want to show off our impact and compassion, we want to show off our creativity and expressiveness, and we want to build a large community to demonstrate our social prowess.

We are now beginning to see the emergence of Internet 3.0. While 1.0 took us online and 2.0 created new value through networks, the new generation of the web is about delivering human-scale solutions. These new models, largely created by Millennials, harness the power of the Internet to make it possible to reconnect to ourselves, each other, and our communities by harnessing the power of relationships. The Internet has created a platform that has made it so easy to find people, products, and services that in a sense, we are able to create the village again—though this time, we are not limited by our geography or social class.

Before the rise of technology, work and consumption were personal. We bought food and products directly from the people in our community that grew and built them. We shared resources with our neighbors. When we traveled, we stayed in local inns or with strangers who had a room to rent. We read the news in a local paper written by local writers. At this scale, suppliers knew the people who used their goods and services, and customers knew who created the products and services they used.

The Industrial and Information economies were all about scale and efficiency. Business was almost myopic, focused almost entirely on gaining market share and developing systems that would increase their margins. The result was the proliferation and growth of massive organizations that sold mass-produced commodities and employed people as if they were de facto commodities. In an effort to be more efficient and to optimize for scale, companies sacrificed the humanity behind their products and services.

We are starting to see a return to a personal scale—this time enabled, rather than disrupted, by technology. The third generation of the web allows us to once again have human-scale markets. We are now able to share cars and bikes, stay the night at a home rather than a hotel, buy handmade goods, and even print our own products with a 3-D printer. We can find services provided by people in our own neighborhood, read blogs by neighbors in our own community, and borrow money from like-minded people rather than big banks. The technology that created a scale so large as to drown us has now enabled a scale anchored in people's need for purpose and meaning in their work and lives. It is right-sizing, to steal the term back from big business.

From TaskRabbit to Elance, technology is changing the way we can earn a living, but also changing the way employers think about labor. More than 17 percent of the fourteen million self-employed workers in the United States consider themselves independent contractors or freelancers.[1] Fractional Labor, as it sometimes called, is concentrated heavily in sales, IT, creative services, marketing, and operations. As Generation X and Millennials have entered the workforce, more professionals of their generations (and even older) have been seeking alternative ways to do work that is meaningful, powered by Internet 3.0. The technology pipeline, from better 3-D printing to robotics to big data, will likely only further accelerate these changes.

2. The Maslow Millennial Effect

While many generations have sought out purpose, Millennials make it a greater priority than ever before, in everything from their consumption to their work to their communities to their relationships.

Arthur Woods, a 2010 graduate of Georgetown University, was excited when he landed a job at Google, the most desired employer of graduating college students, according to Forbes.[2] He had heard the stories and loved what he learned, particularly the fact that every employee was able to dedicate 20 percent of their time to passion projects. Google was a force for building good infrastructure, making information accessible, and connecting people. The best part was that employees who went against the grain were rewarded, rather than punished, for their bold creativity.

By the time he graduated, Arthur had already started a business and a very successful nonprofit, Compass Fellowship, that had spread to 18 universities across the country. Google would provide the corporate experience he needed, while enabling him to remain creative and entrepreneurial. He would be semi-autonomous and have fluid roles that offered the clear opportunity to create social progress and impact in the world. He would be challenged and have a strong community that would push him to do amazing work.

After joining Google, Arthur found the reality to be very different. Like all companies with thousands of employees, Google struggled to fully enable their youngest hires with meaningful opportunities and roles within the organization. Though Arthur was sitting in the heart of Google in Silicon Valley, he could have just as easily been in a call center for a utility company in any anonymous office park. The job consisted of 30 hours per week of mainly rote roles. The remaining hours were spent in meetings talking about the rote tasks; there was little creative freedom or clear purpose to the work. The only difference was that his peers were also over-achievers and brilliant individuals who shared his vision of Google when they had started.

Being highly social, Arthur used his network to connect to colleagues in the YouTube division and started volunteering for them. After he lobbied for five arduous months for a transfer, they ultimately created a new role for him. Arthur is a classic example of the Millennial workforce: entrepreneurial, ambitious, and socially-oriented. The Millennial generation (those born in the 1980s and 1990s) has become known as the purpose generation. It is increasingly a generation known for its desire to make a difference, grow, and share its passion with the world.[3]

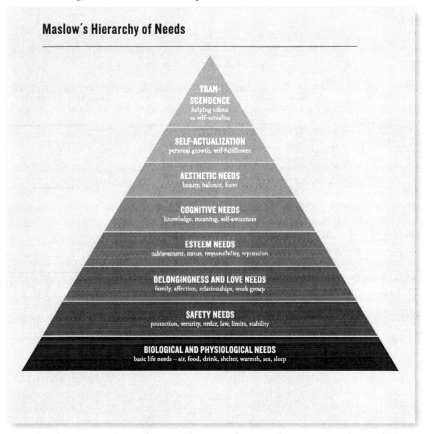

Maslow's Hierarchy of Needs

Abraham Maslow famously put forward a pyramid model to explain human motivations, in which basic survival needs form the base, and others, such as self-esteem and creative expression, only become concerns, or needs, when the more basic ones are satisfied. That this set of priorities is being expressed so powerfully by the Millennials is a natural result of a larger social shift that's been taking place, a shift up Maslow's hierarchy of needs. What is striking about Maslow's hierarchy in relation to the emergence of the Purpose Economy is that it offers a powerful explanation for one reason the economy continues to evolve, and why the aspiration to become more purposeful is now a core motivation for so many people who are lucky enough to live in the developed Information Economy.

Before the 19th century, most of the population was largely focused on survival: getting food to the table was the core economic force. The Industrial Revolution brought greater prosperity, demanding a more educated workforce, and for many, the focus began to shift away from the most basic needs to quality-of-life issues like love, belonging, and esteem. First empowered by the new affluence of the industrial era and then later by the emergence of the Information Economy, an unprecedented portion of the general population was able to focus on the life of the mind, creativity, problem solving, and the discovery and analysis of facts.

Many Westerners in generations X and Y have now reached a level of fulfillment in that regard; we're living lives that keep our minds rigorously engaged in those pursuits. If this evolution continues, more of us will likely be engaged in the next logical step of pursuing lives driven by the fulfillment of higher order needs, such as the need to realize our potential—to become, in Maslow's terms, self-actualized. We now desire to transcend our own needs and prioritize the needs of all of society and future generations, seeking more connection and self-expression. The Purpose Economy is fundamentally fueled by our pursuit of the fulfillment of these needs; the needs themselves have become an economic force.

But how do Millennials differ from other generations? One important way is how they approach work. Whereas the Baby Boomers and Gen X "divorced" their professional lives from personal and civic arenas, Millennials have blurred the line between professional development and personal self-expression (for example, using social media to deliberately leverage their individuality) and eagerly seek out to reconcile their personal values and desire to serve others in a professional setting. Millennials were raised to believe that "they can be whatever they want to be" and don't want to settle for a less-than-meaningful life. In a major study of Millennials, the Pew Research Center recently concluded: "Whatever toll a recession, a housing crisis, a financial meltdown and a pair of wars may have taken on the national psyche in the past few years, it appears to have hit the old harder than the young.... Millennials [are] confident, self-expressive, liberal, upbeat and open to change."[4]

Millennials were not only born into a world of much more perceived affluence than prior generations, but also into one in which these values and aspirations were gaining traction. Inspiring examples of Purpose Economy achievements could be seen all around them. As they came of age, the environmental movement was going mainstream; pioneering social entrepreneurs were popularizing the idea of "doing well by doing good," with forerunners like Paul Hawken of Smith & Hawken, Ben & Jerry's, and Anita Roddick of the Body Shop popularizing a new ethic of corporate social responsibility. Meanwhile, celebrities like Matt Damon, Angelina Jolie, and George Clooney were popularizing a new ethic of individual engagement, making it cool to be socially engaged.

The excesses of Wall Street, the dot-com boom and bust, and the mentality that "greed is good" began to change the scope of the American Dream for many Millennials coming of age. Even as they saw their parents working harder and spending less time at home in order to afford the big house, three cars, and all the accoutrements of success, they were mostly turned off by these status symbols and began to challenge existing paradigms of success. According to a 2013 study by Deloitte, corporate employees (not just Millennials) now believe that the top responsibility of a company is to provide goods and services that positively impact society. This change doesn't revolve around just one generation, but Millennials are certainly a major accelerant.

3. Generation Disrupt

> Generation X entered the workforce during the dot-com boom and was trained to think big and use technology. They are now the generation in charge and are putting those talents to practice working on big purpose.

Many of the pioneers of the Purpose Economy come from Silicon Valley. My peers in Generation X have played a decisive role in crafting the new models for social innovation, in large part because we were at the heart of the rapid-fire growth of the Information Economy in those years. This growth enabled people to obtain incredible amounts of professional experience early in life, which inspired them to continue on to bold and remarkable careers.

The effect of the dot-com boom on Generation X was something akin to that of World War II on the Baby Boomer generation. My grandfather, for example, was given the opportunity to play a critical role in post-war Germany as a member of the Four Power Allied Control Council, which controlled Germany after its defeat. Though he was still only in his twenties, the war accelerated my grandfather's career and gave him a great sense of hope for what might be possible. He would go on to work in the State Department in helping to form the United Nations, develop the blueprint for the Peace Corps, and run both the Salk and Aspen Institutes. An impressive career trajectory to be sure, but one not likely possible at any other time or in any other place.

I was lucky enough to be in the Bay Area during the dot-com craze, and one of my first jobs was for a small start-up called

HomeShark.com, which sought to empower homeowners and buyers in making better real estate decisions; that is, to upend the traditional model of the industry and put the control back into the hands of the consumer. I then took a job as a product manager for a start-up called iSyndicate, a pioneer in developing the new form of journalism that would eventually evolve into blogging.

I left the dot-com world with a keen understanding of the power of technology, and how one website could upset a market or could connect two people who would have never otherwise met. Even my peers who didn't work in technology were intoxicated by the potential and the realization that in spite of our youth and lack of experience, with the right idea and know-how, we could fundamentally change the way things had worked. Not only did I get the equivalent of a hands-on MBA, but as so many of us did, I saw the extraordinary power of the web for those who came up with the right idea and followed through on it with the right passion.

Our goals in those days may not have been as noble as helping a country recover from the devastation of war—many dot-coms were frivolous misadventures—but we had seen what could be done by one person and an idea, with the help of technology. Groundbreaking change was possible. And as the dot-com sector regained its footing after the crash, we saw whole industries transformed, as well as the way most Americans communicated and engaged in society.

So many of the pioneers in social entrepreneurship, social media, and sustainability are from Generation X and were in some way engaged with the dot-com boom. Jimmy Wales and Larry Sanger of Wikipedia, Max Levchin, Elon Musk and Peter Thiel of PayPal, and Chris Anderson of Wired and now 3DRobotics are just a few examples. The core leadership of the Purpose Economy today is from this often forgotten generation, who in many ways produced the architects and catalysts of the new economy.

4. Environmental, Economic & Political Turmoil

> The growing uncertainty in our society is moving people to find stability within themselves, and to identify the need, to develop empathy for those affected by turmoil.

Amy Wrzesniewski was teaching at New York University during the 9/11 tragedy. A few days after the attack, classes resumed. To her surprise, nearly every student attended, and they were deeply engaged, but not in the curriculum she had planned. They talked about the tragedy and what could be done. Many were in tears and deeply rattled. Amy realized it would be ludicrous to lecture them about how to maximize team performance in organizations that day or for many days to come.

She, like many of her peers in universities and working in research, struggled to understand the value of her work in the context of seeing the horror of 9/11. Many searched for new projects to help connect their backgrounds to something that would make sense of what had happened, or at least help them find meaning in it.

Amy herself became curious about how people changed their approach to work when the significance of it was called into question by tragedy. She had seen all the news stories of individuals who changed course and found new work that they perceived to be of greater service to humanity. She found major increases in enrollment in service roles, from teaching to the military.[5] "Rather than focusing on extrinsic job concerns, the terrorist attacks caused many people to ask if they ought to reframe their work lives." People had awakened to their need for purpose.

9/11 wasn't the only tragedy to awaken this need for purpose. The disasters of the last fifteen years, from 9/11 to Hurricane

Katrina to the Great Recession, changed the course of many lives. They caused an especially rude awakening for Millennials, who experienced them during their formative years.

My cousin, Liana Elliott, fell in love the first time she visited New Orleans and knew that it was where she wanted to go to college. She wanted to be in a small city with a vibrant music scene, and New Orleans and Tulane University fit the bill perfectly. Just like her, it was quirky, authentic, and creative, and as an aspiring music journalist she found it far more inspiring than her hometown of Palo Alto.

During her junior year, Hurricane Katrina hit. "[It] literally changed everything," she tells people. She evacuated to Texas as the storm neared and followed the chaos on TV. Liana vividly recalls watching a reporter standing in the parking lot where she worked and seeing in the background, engulfed in flames, the Subway restaurant she had frequented on lunch breaks. As the firemen were trying to douse the flames, there was gunfire, and the reporter and crew ducked and started running. As she told me, "For a white kid from Palo Alto, that wasn't something I was used to seeing in my backyard." It was a shocking thing for anyone to see, but for a sheltered young woman from Palo Alto, it was deeply unsettling.

Liana now describes her life as being "divided into pre- and post-Katrina." Life lessons she had learned as a child about volunteering, being involved with her community, and environmental sustainability became very real. Once Tulane reopened, she returned to New Orleans, only to find her home with no electricity, mail service, or trash pickup. Her blow-up mattress had to be hauled downstairs to her neighbor's FEMA trailer to be re-inflated every night. She showered at the gym, rented a mailbox downtown, and carried a powerstrip to class so she could charge everything all at once. It was challenging, but nothing compared to so many others who had loved ones killed or their livelihoods washed away.

Liana found it hard to remain in school. She wanted to start helping put the city back together and to be involved in the rebuilding and rebirth of the place she had grown to love. She couldn't comprehend the rationale for writing yet another paper for a professor to skim and grade, when there was clearly such need surrounding her in New Orleans. It felt pointless, and like such a waste of time, money, and energy that could be better spent helping the recovery.

Liana did graduate, but no longer with an aspiration to be a music journalist—she had the bug. After seeing the terror of Katrina and the systemic failure of the government and other institutions in preparing for it and in the recovery, she wanted to ensure such travesty didn't happen to New Orleans or any other city again. After graduating, she found work in a local nonprofit working on the recovery and eventually returned to graduate school to study disaster planning and relief.

The disasters of the last fifteen years have profoundly impacted our priorities. Hurricanes Katrina and Sandy, the Deep Horizon oil spill, the visible campaigns against modern-day slavery, and the terrifying news of the rapidly melting polar ice caps have made the fragility of our planet painfully clear. The threat is no longer distant; we no longer look outside our immediate communities to see people suffering devastating consequences from our warming climate, the scarcity of freshwater, or the infiltration of our reservoirs by toxic wastes. The threats are omnipresent.

The economic disaster and housing crisis of 2008—the "Great Recession"—has also forced many people and companies to change their behavior as consumers and employers. The impact of this recession still isn't entirely clear, but Millennials, who came of age in this reality, developed a different set of priorities in response to this new context. Visa reported that the use of debit cards has surpassed that of credit cards, indicating a shifting comfort with debt from previous generations. Millennials have become more creative in finding ways to meet their needs that don't rely on acquiring debt or increasing consumption. Instead, they are finding value in serving others, expressing themselves, and joining communities with shared interests.

Out of great disasters, whether environmental or economic, often come great opportunities. They inspire courage, invention, and innovation. They also force us to redefine normal. We are seeing marvelously inventive new solutions emerging all around us; new models are being tested, hybrid styles of organization are being invented, and capital from both the private sector and the government is being redirected to the Purpose Economy. And this change isn't just coming from Millennials. Their parents, many of whom are reaching retirement, are instead choosing second careers and redefining what it means to age.

5. Longevity

> As they map out their next 30 years, Boomers are designing their second careers and again prioritizing the purpose they sought in their youth. In the process, they inspire the rest of us.

This reimagining of retirement is directly tied to the fact that humans are now living longer than ever. The Baby Boomer generation, now entering traditional retirement age, is trying to reconcile the reality that many will end up living a decade or more longer than their own parents.[6] Unfortunately for many, the recession and increased health care costs have meant pushing off retirement or finding part-time work to cover their needs. Whatever the catalyst, they are making purpose a priority in their second careers.

After working for decades in jobs focused primarily on earning, Boomers are looking for ways to give back and do work that has meaning. As Encore.org, an online platform for helping people find meaningful second careers, articulates, they see their second careers as an opportunity to make some of their most important contributions to themselves, to their families, and to the world. For many, this marks a return to an earlier, more socially-oriented time in their lives. Boomers grew up during the era of some of the most important social movements in our nation's history and were behind many of them, serving on the front lines of the civil rights movement and enduring the pain of the Vietnam War. Many went on to have families and join the corporate ranks, but with their kids leaving the nest, they are reevaluating their priorities and exploring more rewarding opportunities.

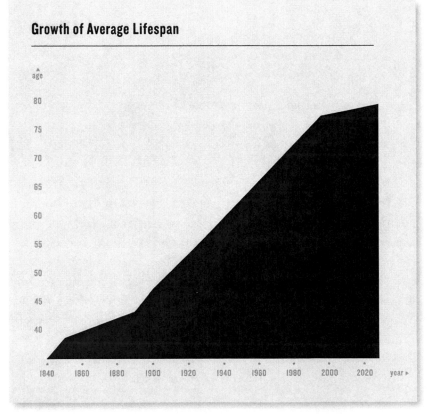

Growth of Average Lifespan

Compared to the generations that came before them, Boomers are more educated, healthier, wealthier, and more inclined to stay in the workforce longer. But for many, that work isn't motivated by the same things it was when they were at their peak earning potential, and it's creating a talent boom for the social sector. Already, Encore.org reports, nine million Boomers are in purpose-rich second careers, with another 31 million seeking them out. They are finding purpose in many places, including education (30%), health care (25%), government (25%), and nonprofit organizations (11%).[7]

My own father, Peter Hurst, became a social entrepreneur in his 60s. After spending the previous few decades of his career in higher education, he became interested in the local school district where he lived and saw an opportunity to make a real impact in his own backyard. Twice a day at suburban schools across the country, cars idle in front as parents drop off and pick up their kids. Kids are not only missing the health benefits of walking or biking to school; the fumes of the idling cars make the air quality around the school closer to that of a bar in Bangkok. To address this issue, he created a program, the Boulder Valley School District's Trip Tracker, which makes walking, biking, busing, and carpooling to school cool and safe again. Last year, they estimate they reduced 300,000 miles of driving and over 10,000 gallons of gas use in 12 schools.[8] He has told me that despite the low pay and prestige, it is the job he has enjoyed most over the last 50 years.

Other Baby Boomers are finding a solution not in changing their vocation or starting new programs, but through involvement in their community as volunteers, board members, and donors. Boomers now collectively donate over $60 billion per year to charity.[9] The number of volunteers age 65 and older in the U.S. will increase 50 percent by 2020, from just under 9 million in 2007 to over 13 million.[10] These numbers demonstrate that the social engagement we are seeing from seniors is not simply a trend or a passing fad, but a fundamental shift in Americans' changing views of retirement and what it means to grow old.

This goes beyond Boomers, as watching this happen to the Boomers makes all the rest of us realize that we'll be working a lot longer, or maybe never really retiring. If you're looking at working 55 to 60 years of your life, you're going to want that time to be enjoyable and meaningful.

6. Changing Families and Evolving Roles

> Both parents in most families now work, and one of the many consequences of this change is that we are hiring people in record numbers for the jobs highest in purpose—caring for our kids and aging parents.

We are now living longer, starting our families later, and often marrying more than once—dynamics that are drastically changing the nature and structure of families in the United States. While not unheard of, these were certainly anomalies when my grandmother was coming of age in the 1920s. She worked for a few years before she married, but then mostly focused her energy on supporting my grandfather and raising my mother and her sister. My mother and her sister then created hybrid lives that brought in some income, but also enabled them to focus a significant amount of time on home. My wife Kara and I both have full-time jobs that require both of us to work long hours, in addition to parenting our two young children and taking care of the house. Recently, after an especially long week, Kara joked in a moment of clarity and frustration that she needed a "wife." She was, of course, referring to the wife of our grandmother's generation.

We are not alone. 82 percent of women in the United States now work, a 250 percent increase since the 1950s.[11] Fewer than

7 percent of households have only a male breadwinner.[12] This is a radical change in our households and lives. As the Industrial Economy gave way to the Information Economy, labor transitioned from a physical to an intellectual endeavor, an important factor in opening doors for women to join the workforce in legions. Despite a persistent glass ceiling at the top of most corporations, women have risen to higher-level roles in steadily increasing numbers, and this has contributed to another core driver of the growth of the Purpose Economy.

Economics has historically been a male-dominated profession, and so it is of little surprise that household work was never considered in the calculation of the nation's economic output. The most important and purpose-rich work done in our society was left off the books and devalued. According to the Bureau of Economic Analysis, in 2010 the estimated economic value of household work would have boosted the American GDP by 26 percent.[13] With women unable to devote as much time to household work, we are now outsourcing much of it. The number of preschool teachers is expected to grow by 25 percent between 2010 and 2025, and the number of childcare workers 20 percent in that same time.[14] Once a cottage industry, childcare has started to integrate into corporate models. The day care/preschool Kiddie Academy, for example, has created a successful model that already has franchises in nearly half of the United States.

And yet, this new reality of a more fully integrated workforce is just one of the distinctive features of the decades-long transformation of the Industrial Economy. The fastest-growing part of household outsourcing is in the care of the elderly who, while living longer, are suffering from chronic illnesses that require ongoing attention. Seniors now account for 12.9 percent of the population—a number expected to increase to 20 percent by 2030—and as of 2010, there were approximately 1.9 million home health and personal care aides in the United States to care for them.[15]

The employment of home health aides is projected to grow 60 percent from 2010 to 2020, with the personal care aide profession expected to grow 70 percent.[16] To fill this employment gap, we are seeing a rise in home health and personal care aides, now one of the fastest growing professions in the United States. By enabling seniors to stay at home longer, aides can help to reduce the cost and length of stay in nursing homes, provide companionship, monitor their patients' diets, and ensure they take medications correctly, which can help avoid hospitalization.

Furthermore, as Boomers age (10,000 now reach the age of 65 everyday in the U.S.), they are looking for new senior care solutions, and innovative new ventures are emerging and scaling to meet their needs. Kiran Yocom's Seniors Helping Seniors, for example, has been a pioneer in meeting the non-medical needs of seniors living independently, but in need of companionship and daily activities. Care.com, an online platform to find caretakers for parents or grandparents, boasts over 9.5 million members.[17] Seniors Helping Seniors' innovation was to use more active seniors, often in need of a little income, to serve in these roles. Today, there are 200 franchises operating on this model.

The growth in home health care and other outsourced domestic work is only now beginning to show up in the economy, as well as, I would argue, part of the emerging Purpose Economy. It creates work that is high in potential for meaning and is an important part of our new educational and social services systems.

7. New Social Science

The new field of positive psychology has dispelled many of the myths about success and purpose and is changing the way leaders think.

As the needs of individuals and families have evolved and changed, the advent of a new field of social science has simultaneously emerged. Positive psychology has materialized in the last dozen years to examine the role of meaning and well-being in our lives and at work. Researchers in the field study how human beings prosper in the face of adversity and the conditions necessary for them to flourish.

While the term 'positive psychology' was first coined by Abraham Maslow in the 1950s, it was the University of Pennsylvania's Martin Seligman who popularized the idea in 1998, when he presented it in his presidential address at the annual meeting of the American Psychological Association. He was one of a growing group of leaders in psychology who were unhappy with the disease-oriented field and saw a void when it came to studying positive psychological traits like meaning, courage, and happiness.

In his book *Flourish,* Dr. Seligman argues that happiness is too narrow a conception of the goal we should be shooting for, and that the more rounded, richer condition he calls well-being is the proper aim. While experiencing happiness has obvious value, he points out that happiness is quite a variable element in our lives, and that sometimes in order to achieve our goals, it's simply necessary to forego some happiness. Happiness is, at any rate, generally quite fleeting; it is really a mood rather than a state of being. Well-being, by contrast, is a more enduring condition. Vital to its attainment, Seligman argues, are five core components: positive emotion, engagement, relationships, meaning, and accomplishment.[18]

But well-being isn't just good for people; it's good for business. 21st-century-born organizations like Zappos and Etsy are making investments in measuring and maximizing the well-being of their employees, levering the emerging research of pioneers like Seligman. Matt Stinchcomb, Etsy's Vice President of Values and Impact, partnered with the University of Pennsylvania's Center for Positive Psychology to launch a company-wide study of employee well-being. The team leveraged the PERMA measurement framework—a self-assessment tool developed by Dr. Seligman that quantifies positive emotions, engagement, relationships, meaning, and accomplishment—to gauge the well-being of Etsy employees. Almost 85 percent of Etsy's 400 employees participated, including 24 teams in five offices across five countries. Etsy now uses the data as one of its core success metrics.

Forward-thinking companies aren't the only ones who have embraced this new research and the call to making well-being a priority for their people. The city of Santa Monica recently joined Seattle and the state of Vermont in prioritizing well-being as a core metric for their city's success. It sounds simple, but it radically changes how decisions are made, how the government is held accountable, and how resources are invested.

We are continuing to see the field of research advance with brilliant new minds working on these issues. Adam Grant, Seligman's colleague at the University of Pennsylvania and the youngest-ever tenured professor at Wharton, published his breakthrough research in his 2013 book *Give and Take.*[19] The research draws a direct, first-time correlation between success and giving—not simply in the sense of donations, but more broadly as an approach to relationships. It is an important work and provides the data and research to show why serving others and the greater good isn't just good for the world, but good for your career and for business.

Thought-leading researchers like Adam Grant and Martin Seligman have changed the fundamental approach to management and career development from one of overcoming weaknesses to one of embracing and investing in strengths. They have started to crack the code on how to enable purpose and well-being at work, and their research is now becoming foundational reading for executive coaches and management consultants. This kind of emerging research supports and fuels the changing role of management and leadership to help people find purpose and meaning, rather than just to move up the corporate ladder.

8. Accelerated Globalization

> The world has become a smaller place, and we are inspired by the potential and challenges it holds.

Information technology and air transportation have made the world a village. We have become much more connected to people all over the globe and been made much more aware of the problems so many people in the developing world are coping with. In village life, if you mistreat members of the community or harm the local environment, everyone knows it, and you are subject to intense scrutiny and held accountable. Similarly, as the world has become interconnected, we are no longer so free to look the other way about the impact we're having on people's lives around the globe. We've been brought into a tighter accountability and feedback loop

We get constant first-hand accounts of the suffering in Darfur in a way that was unimaginable fifty years ago. We also see the impact of our irresponsible and unsustainable imperialist practices on poorer countries and cultures. It's become increasingly hard to close our eyes and ears to that devastation and to the inadequacies in so many countries around the globe, from the teeming slums of India to the horrors of Haiti's fragile infrastructure. That awareness has spurred an increasing commitment to take part in making change happen.

Globalization has also brought transformative technologies to the developing world, opening up extraordinary opportunities for rapid social change there. As Thomas Friedman argued in his bestseller *The World Is Flat*, globalization has acted as a leveler of the playing field of business, providing both the impetus and opportunity for those in the developing world to begin to compete with the leading industrial powers.[20] He points out that one of the ironies of the excesses of the dot-com boom was that it led to so much installation of high-speed cable, and with this over-capacity, the costs of entry to the wired world were driven down dramatically.

The technological transformation hardly stopped there. The use of cell phones has grown more rapidly over the past several years in Africa than in the developed world, and mobile banking is becoming an important new force of commerce in many of the developing nations. Mobile phones and the Internet also played an important role in the success of revolutions of the Arab Spring.

Globalization has brought massive change even in the furthest reaches of the planet. In the Gobi desert, Mongolian nomads chat on cell phones and install solar panels next to their yurts. In the most remote villages of Africa, school children are starting to have access to laptops. The combination of the possibilities and the needs that globalization has made apparent has motivated a legion of innovators to create new solutions.

Here in the United States, we understand the need to be globally literate. 93 percent of Americans now believe that international knowledge is important, with three in four favoring college requirements in international courses, language training, and study abroad.[21] We have a long way to go to build that level of literacy in the classroom, but technology is starting to close that gap.

9. A Shifting Social Context

Organizations and individuals are seeing the gap in what the government can accomplish and trying to step in to fill it.

Great Society architect John Gardner's 1964 book *Self-Renewal*, an inspiration for Taproot when I read it years later, eloquently laid out the case that our institutions were beginning to cave under their own weight.[22] For the first time in history, our nation had become dependent on huge government, large companies, and other institutions whose success, scale, and decades of rigidity-forming policies were preventing them from adapting. The United States government is the oldest of its kind, and many of the largest American companies are also among the longest-standing in the world. According to Gardner, these organizations were calcifying, and with them, our ability to thrive as a nation. Trust in the federal government has been on a decline for decades.

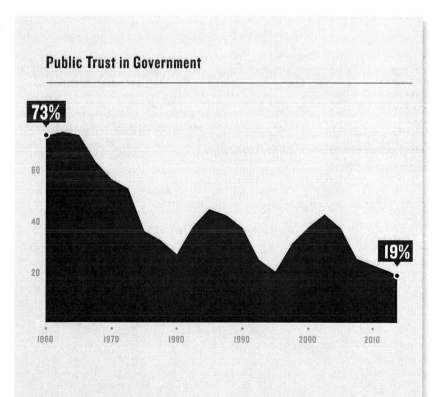

Public Trust in Government

73%

19%

My grandfather had believed that civil service was the highest calling, but it was hard for me to hold this faith growing up in the last two decades of the 20th century. While teaching creative writing at the Cotton Correctional Facility in Jackson, Michigan, I bonded with an inmate named John. He was a college graduate, generally a nice guy, and it wasn't clear to me what he had done to land himself in prison. He could have easily blended in with my friends back on campus at the University of Michigan. But by the time I graduated from Michigan and stopped teaching at Cotton, John was barely recognizable to me. It wasn't that I had turned him into a best-selling author—quite the opposite. He had become indistinguishable from the other hardened prisoners in the room. His language, tone, dress, and attitude had been completely transformed. Like a chameleon that changes color based on its surroundings, John had changed his demeanor and personality to fit into his new life—life in prison.

Witnessing his downward spiral was profoundly upsetting. I had failed him. Prison had turned a good man into someone you wouldn't want to run into in a dark alley. At least on the surface, he was a fundamentally different person. Working with him and other inmates there taught me more than anything else I gained in my four years at Michigan. It was clear that our government was not helping us create a more just society; it was making the situation worse through a short-sighted and poorly designed criminal justice system. The experience taught me that it is much easier to proactively support the Johns of the world before they end up in jail, and it becomes extremely difficult to turn the situation around after incarceration, as recidivism rates consistently demonstrate. Also, volunteer programs like the one at Cotton, which I had helped design and lead, would have to be radically rethought to have any real impact.

The frustration with the prevailing government-dependent approach to tackling social problems came to a head in the early

1980s, when then-President Ronald Reagan gave it voice, famously pronouncing in his 1981 inaugural address that "government is not the solution to our problem; government is the problem." That started the so-called "Reagan Revolution" that sought to put the power and responsibility of society into the hands of individuals and organizations.

In the *Federalist Papers*, James Madison clearly outlined the goal of government as centered on justice. This didn't only apply to a fair court system and rule of law; it was about the justice in bestowing equal treatment and opportunity. It was also clearly defined as caring for those in need. Reagan didn't share this view of government's role, and his statement that government was the problem ushered in a sea of change in American opinion that significantly altered our social contract— but it didn't happen overnight. According to Pew, even in 1987, near the end of Reagan's second term, the majority of Republicans (62 percent) believed that it is the responsibility of the government to take care of people who can't take care of themselves. Today it stands at 40 percent.[24]

As he began to cut social programs, Reagan looked to private organizations, especially nonprofit groups, to pick up the slack for government. He developed the Task Force on Private Sector Initiates explicitly to help transition government responsibilities back to the people through nonprofit organizations. At the time, however, many of the nonprofits that were providing the critical services in question were largely funded by government grants. The new policies not only eliminated the government programs, but also cut the funding for many of the nonprofit programs that would be asked to pick up the slack.

If the services of these nonprofits were important to the community, then the community would fund them. Reagan believed that nonprofits needed to act less like quasi-governmental agencies and begin to behave more like private sector companies, responding to market feedback. He also believed that releasing nonprofits from government constraints would create innovation in the sector as well as new business models to generate revenue that was market-driven.

It took a little over a decade before Americans began to see the impact of the Reagan-era changes. In response to government's diminished role, communities began starting organizations to fill the gap left by government. By 2008, the nonprofit sector was spending $1.34 trillion a year, and two years later it represented 5.4 percent of the nation's GDP.[25] Perhaps more importantly, by 2009, the sector accounted for 10 percent of the jobs in the nation. With this kind of growth comes a need to scale, which requires more sophisticated business skills and more innovative types of organizations.[26] The new hybrid nonprofit and for-profit organizations that have emerged bear many similarities to the organizations serving these functions before them, but they are evolving and becoming increasingly complex—an evolution that will surely continue.

10. Blending of the Sectors

The line between government, nonprofits, and companies is blurring, and every sector is seeing purpose at the core of their future.

The emergence of these new hybrid organizations is one of the most promising developments of the last decade. Sometimes called flexible-purpose corporations, B Corporations, or low-profit limited companies (or L3C), they all combine profit-making with a social mission. The L3C structure facilitates private philanthropic investment in the companies by combining the legal protections and tax benefits of an LLC with the benefits of being a socially oriented nonprofit. This makes L3Cs appealing investments for foundations, as a foundation can further its mission and fulfill its obligation to pay out at least 5% of its endowment every year but also anticipate receiving a return on that investment.[27]

The structure also helps address the problem of the donor-hunting treadmill nonprofits are on, by facilitating their use of profits as a mechanism for attracting donors while protecting them from a tax burden. Traditional nonprofits are not allowed to distribute any profits made from their activities—such as the Girl Scouts' highly successful cookie-selling operation—to funders, or to issue shares or dividends to private funders. The L3C is a brilliant way of using a cross-sector model to add leverage to the philanthropic funding pool and to take some of the fundraising pressure off of nonprofits. But the L3C is still in its infancy. The structure must be approved at the state level and, at the time of this writing, has only been approved by nine states—Illinois, Louisiana, Maine, Michigan, North Carolina, Rhode Island, Utah, Vermont, and Wyoming—as well as the federal jurisdictions of the Crow Indian Nation of Montana and the Oglala Sioux Tribe.

Still, we are starting to see traction with these new hybrid business models. In just a few years, over 750 companies have voluntarily become certified as B Corporations (B Corps). Unlike L3Cs, B Corps have separate legal/no legal status, but volunteer to signal their intent to be for-benefit companies. The advantage to the B Corp is that it can promote itself to investors as a solid opportunity for returns while also allowing them to support a social mission. In a recent article, *Fast Company* called B Corps the "rockstars of the new economy," and prominent companies that have gone the B Corp route include Etsy, Warby Parker, Patagonia, and Seventh Generation. The structure must also be approved by state legislatures, and as of this writing, eleven states have done so, from Maryland to Hawaii.

New investment models are being pioneered as well. Social impact bonds, as described earlier, are another potentially powerful type of hybrid innovation. An interesting approach to this kind of investment blending is being practiced by the Omidyar Network to early stage social entrepreneurs. They offer grants, in the manner of a foundation, as well as loans or equity investments, for which a return is expected. The method of funding is determined according to the model and needs of the organization.

But the blending can happen more organically, too. Take the case of YouTube or Wikipedia. No one is paid to post a video on YouTube, and yet approximately 72 hours of video are uploaded every minute. In some ways, YouTube could be considered the largest volunteer organization in the world. Or consider the rise of citizen journalism, flourishing on sites such as Wikinews and the South Korean OhmyNews, which offers anyone who has knowledge of breaking news events the opportunity to circumvent the biases that can distort so much of commercially-funded news coverage.

Many of the most important markets operate across sectors. American hospitals and schools, for example, are now run by nonprofits, corporations, and governments. According to David Walker, Comptroller General of the United States, as of 2003, 62 percent of hospitals were run by nonprofits, 20 percent by government, and 18 percent were corporate. For-profit colleges represented 3 percent of enrollment in 2002, but nine years later had tripled to 9 percent. And while a single organization or sector can make an impact in a market, to scale from innovation to a tipping point, it is essential to deploy multiple market levers.

For almost every market, the organizations that have the greatest muscle to move levers sit in different sectors. Nonprofits can influence policy, but they don't set it. Inversely, the government can conduct research and change policy, but typically needs to partner with the private sector to change public perceptions or to develop innovations. In other words, to move a market, we have to look beyond sector boundaries.

And as we move beyond sector lines, it is increasingly difficult for business to be able to justify a myopic bottom-line strategy or for nonprofits to ignore the importance of market forces. The silos are being removed by choice and by necessity. What we expect of organizations is changing.

My First Corporate Job

In 1997, my mother's sister, Sandra Slater, lived in Silicon Valley and generously let me crash with her while I searched for a corporate job. From a computer in her guest room, I began applying for jobs, but realized it could take months to land a gig. I pragmatically signed up at a local temp agency to see if I could find some bridge work to help protect my small savings from evaporating.

At an office near Stanford, I took a battery of tests to determine my potential as a temp. My two-finger typing amazed the staff. It was apparently the fastest and most accurate two-finger pecking they had ever seen.

Despite their awe, it wasn't until two weeks later that they called me. It was a Friday afternoon. They had a short-term assignment for me at Comerica Bank in downtown Palo Alto; it started the following Monday. Was I interested and available?

I asked what kind of work it entailed. "Firing." Firing? "Yes, they need some firing done." Silence. OK. "Plan to be at the bank by 9:00 on Monday and just introduce yourself. They will be expecting you." OK. "Have a good weekend and congratulations."

I was in shock. Firing? Things in the business community really are different. Jesus.

I shared the news with my family, who were at some level surprised about the nature of this job, but it was pretty consistent with the corporate America we knew. The news was filled with stories of outsourcing and off-shoring. Companies were machines run by emotionless robot-like executives.

It was flattering, to be honest. In college, I had taken several courses in organization and team dynamics that were listed on my resumé. They must have also seen my nonprofit experience as a sign of my compassion and empathetic skills.

By the end of the day Saturday, I was starting to get my head around it. Firing sucks for the manager and the person being fired. It was so personal, awkward and embarrassing. Bringing in someone from the outside takes some of the sting out and prevents it from becoming personal.

They would likely set me up in an office and then just tell employees they needed to come meet with me. I would share the hard news and let them know it was the company's decision and it was final. They couldn't fight me on it as I was just a temp. They might cry. I decided I would need to be compassionate and just sit and listen as a neutral stranger. They would find another job. Don't give up. Eventually they would leave, get their things, and exit.

By mid-day Sunday, everyone in my family knew about my temp job at Comerica Bank. It was not good PR for the business community. They tried to balance their scorn for Comerica

Bank with their pride in my for being selected for this tough assignment.

On Sunday night, a new dilemma emerged. What should I wear to work the next day? Like a teenage girl, I must have tried on every outfit I owned. With each, I looked in the mirror and tried to imagine what it would be like to be fired by someone in that suit combination. Black would show respect, but was it too somber? This wasn't a funeral, just a speed bump in their careers. But if I went the other direction and wore bright colors, it might come across as flippant.

Ultimately, I got in my car Monday morning in a dark suit with a warm tie and headed to work. My palms were cold and sweaty as I made the 15-minute drive.

As instructed, I reported to the front desk and they sent me to meet with the HR manager. It was time to get trained on the firing process apparently. I took a deep breath.

After a few pleasantries about the weekend, the HR manager pointed to the far right corner of the floor where I would be doing the FILING. A backlog of wills and trusts had accumulated when a member of the team went on maternity leave. I was to spend the week filing them alphabetically by last name.

Equal parts embarrassed and relieved, I walked to the far right of the floor, began with the As, and worked my way through the alphabet by the end of the week.

SECTION TWO
PERSONAL PURPOSE—OWNING IT

PURPOSE IS ALL ABOUT HOW
YOU APPROACH YOUR WORK

PURPOSE ISN'T A CAUSE,   REVELATION,   OR LUXURY.

PURPOSE IS A CHOICE.

4
Purpose Is What Matters

"The man without purpose is like a ship without a rudder—waif, a nothing, a no man."—Thomas Carlyle (1795–1881)

How is success defined? For many of us, we focus on what we can most easily measure: money. Money does matter, of course, at least until we reach a "comfortable standard." We need a certain level of income to be able to meet our basic needs and remove acute levels of stress. Researchers at Princeton compared Gallup data on the income and happiness of 500,000 American households. They found that after about $75,000, money had no impact on mood.[1] In a household with two earners, that equals under $40,000 per year (obviously higher in markets like New York City).

But this isn't news. By now we all know that the person who dies with the most toys isn't necessarily the most successful. Philosophers, clergy, and in more recent times, economists and psychologists, have written endless amounts of books on this topic. It remains one of the most written-about topics, and most writings consistently note that money is not core to the meaning of life. So, what matters?

The roots of the conversation appear to go back to Aristotle, who described mere happiness as a vulgar idea. He observed that while many behaviors might produce pleasure, they do not produce well-being, or what he called *eudaimonia*. Feeling good is a brief and fleeting experience, and is not enough to sustain a good life.

Dr. Martin E.P. Seligman from the University of Pennsylvania picked up where Aristotle left off with his theory of well-being. Seligman is one of the leaders in the new field of positive psychology and the author of the book *Flourish*.[2] According to Seligman, what we should seek to achieve is well-being, not simply happiness, which he sees as being one-dimensional and fleeting. Seligman breaks down well-being into five areas: positive emotion, engagement, relationships, meaning, and accomplishment, or PERMA.

Positive emotion is the basis for having a pleasant life, and includes things like warmth and pleasure—things we associate with basic happiness. Borrowing from the work of Mihaly Csikszentmihalyi, he also describes how you can be in a state of "flow," when you lose a sense of self-consciousness and are operating with all your mental and emotional powers. This level of engagement, he shares, requires deploying your highest strengths and talents. The element of meaning typically goes beyond what he describes as the often solitary experiences of positive emotions and engagement. Meaning is about who we are and how we are in the world. It is about more than the here and now, and it is about more than just the self.

So, how does this all play out in life? Some of the most interesting writing and research in this area has focused on parenting.[3] Being a parent—and especially a single parent, it turns out—is negatively correlated with a traditional sense of pleasure or happiness. Studies show that people with kids report far less pleasure in their lives than their childless counterparts. This is 100 percent consistent with my experience and those of every parent I know. Parenting kicks your ass. But being a parent is also the most important part of my life, and I wouldn't trade my life for those of my childless friends (well, not for more than a week anyway). Parenting is profoundly meaningful and rewarding; it is, however, rarely engaging or pleasurable.

In an attempt to understand the relationship between the five components of well-being, British academics Mathew P. White and Paul Dolan asked people to assess different activities based on the degree of pleasure and reward they received from doing them.[3] The winner? Volunteerism. It was the highest rated activity for both pleasure (i.e., positive emotion and engagement) and reward (i.e., meaning).

Having worked in pro bono service for over a dozen years, this came as no surprise to me. Volunteering your time is profoundly rewarding and pleasurable. However, I also learned that pro bono, the donation of your highest strengths and talents, was more rewarding and pleasurable than traditional volunteerism, because it combines the elements of meaning and engagement. As John Gardner wrote, "True happiness involves the full use of one's power and talents."[4]

One of the quotes I shared in the first chapter from a Taproot pro bono consultant sums up this ideal perfectly: "My passion for helping people is rivaled only by my passion for automating things with computers. I want to combine these two things." He wants to combine meaning and engagement, and he is seeking to do pro bono service to achieve a sense of purpose.

When we combine meaning with engagement, we find the pinnacle state of purpose, where our well-being is highest and most sustained. It turned out that pro bono service was a great supplement for people who weren't obtaining the level of meaning they needed in their lives.

> "I always think that's one of the great myths—that you separate [yourself] in business."
>
> —Anita Roddick, Founder, The Body Shop

Supplements are sometimes necessary, but more important is adjusting our lives to have more integrated ways to sustain

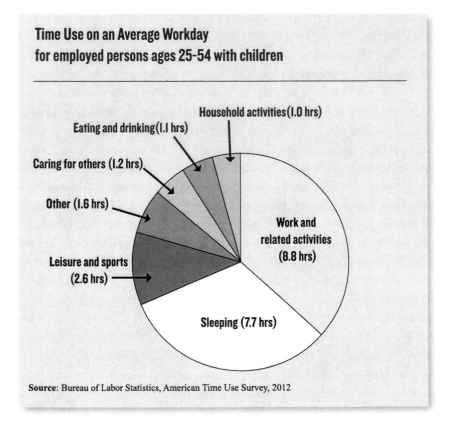

**Time Use on an Average Workday
for employed persons ages 25-54 with children**

Household activities(1.0 hrs)

Eating and drinking(1.1 hrs)

Caring for others (1.2 hrs)

Other (1.6 hrs)

Work and related activities (8.8 hrs)

Leisure and sports (2.6 hrs)

Sleeping (7.7 hrs)

Source: Bureau of Labor Statistics, American Time Use Survey, 2012

ourselves. During the week, most of us spend at least 50 percent of our waking time at work. If we aren't getting our need for purpose met here, we are unlikely to have satisfying levels of purpose in our overall lives. Purpose enables us to thrive; we need it in the activity we spend most of our waking hours doing: working.

Work is core to our well-being. To illustrate this on a small scale, the General Society surveyed Americans and asked how many would quit their jobs if they suddenly came upon a fortune that guaranteed a life of luxury until their last day. Nearly three-quarters of Americans stated they would not quit their job. Americans who feel they are successful at work are twice as likely to say they are very happy overall as people who don't feel that way.[5]

> "Happiness lies not in the mere possession of money; it lies in the joy of achievement, in the thrill of creative effort."
>
> — Franklin D. Roosevelt

What Happens to a Dream Deferred?

Tom Eddington was a partner at Hewitt Associates. He had been one of its early employees and had just moved from London, where he helped to expand its footprint into Europe. He was revered by his team and by his clients. He did good work for organizations, and he was proud of the work they were doing in the world. He had a beautiful family and an impressive paycheck from Hewitt every two weeks. If you asked anyone about him, they would immediately share that he was a 'good guy' and a respected leader.

That was the Tom I knew when I met him in the course of partnering with Hewitt to build up our human resources practice at Taproot. He had agreed to be our executive champion, pilot our first projects in the area, and ultimately join our board. He was bullish on the need for pro bono in the HR community.

It was at this time that something dramatically changed his life. Years before, he had lived in Connecticut and had been bitten by a tick, and he was just now starting to experience symptoms of Lyme disease. It wasn't clear at first what was going on, but after meeting with doctors all around the country, he was able to get a diagnosis—and it was a scary one. Tom's whole world turned upside down. He had to take leave from his post at Hewitt and focus on getting better. He started to see his life falling apart all around him. He had focused so much of his life on his career, and now it was all disintegrating. He had been raised to see success rooted in money and status, and that had driven how he presented himself to the world. But now, it wasn't clear if he would ever be able to work again.

As he describes it, "everything just kind of melted away," giving him the opportunity to start to make conscious choices with clarity. He struggled with what to do with all these thoughts and feelings and began to channel them into his work with Taproot.

Through his pro bono work, Tom was exposed to the indigent and the broader needs of the community, alongside a team of peers who were having similar awakenings. He recalls one member of his team who had been a very successful professional and suddenly found himself out of work, struggling with his identity after being stripped of his title and position. He was very talented, but was losing his self-confidence. He was stuck, but in his work with the pro bono team, he began to get his confidence back and to connect to a broader purpose.

It took five years for Tom to take control of his health and to begin to have a strong self-identity that was not rooted in his childhood, expectations of others, or traditional career success. He would be the first to say that he isn't 100 percent there yet, but he has reached a tipping point. He has realized that his education and mentoring as a leader had left him without the most important asset he needed to try to be successful—consciousness.

Learn, Earn & Return

During a recent TED talk, moral philosopher Peter Singer argued that the best way to change the world is to go into finance. You can make a lot of money and then give it away. If you make enough, you can pay the salaries of dozens of aid workers, which has a better social return on investment than simply becoming an aid worker yourself. And the best part is that you get rich, too.

This is the fable of "learn, earn, and then return". It was first introduced to me by Toni La Belle when she was managing director at Lehman Brothers. Toni and I met when I was working to open the Taproot office in New York City. She had been a corporate powerhouse for decades and had recently begun to become active in the social sector through board service. Like her peers, Toni had been raised on the learn, earn, and then return model. The framework was heavily promoted by the former CEO of Metronics, Bill George. After retiring, George joined the faculty at Harvard's business school. His course, True North, which sought to help develop the soft skills of students, quickly became the most popular course at the business school. His book of the same name outlines the learn, earn, and return model and how it has been the executive blueprint for decades.

The thinking goes something like this. You spend the first 30 years of your life "rubbing up against the world." The first third of your life is spent learning skills and about yourself, as you gain new experiences to help identify your path. The second third of your life is when you are in the heart of your earning potential and serving as a leader. You begin to step up into leadership positions, and by your fifties you are at your peak. The final third of your life is focused on giving back. It is when you reinvest in future generations and the world. As Bill George described, it is a time when leaders serve on boards and focus on sharing their wisdom with future generations through teaching, mentoring, and coaching.

Shaping a New Model

Apt as it may have been for another time, the "learn, earn, and then return" model is inadequate for today. It no longer fits our society or the needs of new generations. A more useful and frankly gratifying model is to blend all three into every year of your career. We must constantly be learning, earning, and returning. Continual learning is a constant of successful careers, and many of those who wait to give back never get there. And even if they do, they miss 30 or 40 years of the pleasure of living with a guiding larger purpose.

Jennifer Benz is the poster child for this new model. She is in her mid-thirties and has been able to proactively blend learning, earning, and returning into her work. This is a conscious practice that ensures balance. She is one of the happiest and most purpose-rich people I have the honor of knowing.

Jennifer runs a benefits communication agency. She started it in 2006, and the success of the business has landed her on the top small business list in San Francisco, as well as on *Inc.* magazine's annual rankings. She is also proudly among the largest women-owned firms in the Bay Area. She isn't making "Google" or "Apple" money, but she is making good money (as is her team) and building equity in a thriving business. The part of her work that she loves most is the constant learning. With all the changes in health care, she has to be constantly on her toes and adapting to serve her clients—it is her job to know the field better than anyone. That, coupled with learning how to run a business, has her constantly challenged and growing. Every year, she has major new learning curves to climb, both inside and outside her agency.

Employee benefits communication may not sound like a high-impact field, but Jennifer has seen the difference it can make and deeply believes she is making a critical impact in people's lives. Large employers spend millions on benefits for employees, and many of them go unused or underused. Most companies are terrible at explaining their benefits to employees, and as a result, employees often are unaware or confused about their options. Jennifer finds her purpose renewed when she holds focus groups or interviews with employees. People often feel overwhelmed by health and financial decisions. They truly appreciate and find comfort in the unbiased education and support their employer can provide, and it results in better decisions and long-term outcomes for everyone.

She also finds tremendous purpose in being an advocate for employees in the employee benefits industry, where she has become an influential leader. It is an industry run by insurance and financial services companies, and most of the leaders are men 20 years her senior. As an activist and a younger woman, she is able to help bring key issues to the table that end up impacting the lives of tens of millions of people.

But for Jennifer, that isn't enough. She is deeply involved in the lives of her employees and commits the firm and herself to considerable pro bono work. They do work for Text4Baby to support large-scale public health campaigns, and Jennifer serves on multiple community boards. She also travels around the world volunteering for low-income community health care providers. These commitments push her to stay focused on impact and maintain perspective. She has not only found ways to design her work to learn, earn, and return simultaneously; she has made each part an amplifier for the others. Balancing them actually increases all three, rather than depleting any one. She learns by returning. She returns by earning. It is a virtuous cycle.

It is important to appreciate what Jennifer has done by fully integrating these parts of her work at the same time. The new narrative presents a concept that we shouldn't wait to revisit at age 60, but rather integrate into our careers from the start and throughout our lives.

Pattern Recognition

Amy Wrzesniewski teaches a course for MBA students at Yale's School of Management, with the aim of helping them more thoughtfully navigate their careers. It is a powerful course that requires an enormous amount of self-reflection on the part of her students. She often ends up holding office hours with many of them, becoming their de facto career coach.

Yale attracts students that tend to be purpose-oriented, and it is rare that a student enters the course without the intention to make an impact in the world. What Amy finds, however, is that these students often plan to defer purpose in their careers until after they have done their stint at Goldman Sachs. They will amass some money for half a dozen years and then commit themselves to purpose.

To push back on her students, Amy has them envision their lives in six years, working somewhere like Goldman Sachs. "You are in a serious relationship now. Do you see yourself married by then? Will you have kids? Will they be in private school with the other kids of Goldman employees? How is your spouse going to feel about taking them out of that school when you quit? How are they going to feel about the sudden drop in quality of life? Are you really going to do it?"

It is the same dilemma many lawyers fall into. They enter law school focused on social justice and impact, and then end up paying off debt by working at a big firm doing corporate law and making big dollars. Soon they are addicted, and their purpose is put into deep freeze.

But as I discuss later in this section, the answer isn't necessarily to not take jobs on Wall Street or at a prestigious law firm. Jennifer Benz didn't become a nun and take a vow of poverty. She brought purpose to where she was working, and rather than setting her back, it propelled her forward.

The Gift of Purpose

In case you need more motivation to make purpose a priority in your work today, a recent study from the University of Michigan provides one of the most compelling arguments yet. Your approach to work will most likely be inherited by your children. They won't necessarily adopt your purpose, but they are much more likely to approach work with a priority put on purpose.

When I learned about this piece of research, I reflected on my own experience. Everyone in my family approaches work as a calling. I then began asking people I know, folks who approach their work as a calling, about their families. Nearly everyone stated that both their parents had a calling orientation.

That means that by making the hard but rewarding effort to infuse purpose into your work, you are not only improving your own well-being, but also that of your children. By likely extension, you are impacting their children and their children's children. And there, you have a pretty compelling purpose for working with purpose.

5
Purpose Myth-Busting

"Wait a minute—what's happening to my special purpose!?"—The Jerk, *1979*

So, how do you maximize purpose in your job? Fortunately, there is an increasing amount of research on this topic, which helps create a sound path for making it happen. At the core is the understanding that not everyone derives purpose from the same things, and that you must come to discover your own purpose. Most of what we understand about purpose at work comes from Hollywood. Stories are a powerful way to learn, but most of the stories we see on a screen give us a romanticized view of the role of purpose in our work. They build myths about purpose that actually make it harder for us to focus on what matters. But perhaps the most unfortunate aspect of these myths is that they imply that purpose is not something for everyone, which—based on my experience working with thousands of professionals, as well as emerging research on the topic—couldn't be further from the truth.

Let's get myth-busting!

Myth One: Purpose = Cause

In working with thousands of professionals seeking purpose, the greatest barrier has been the ubiquitous belief that they have to find their cause. When business professionals leave Taproot's pro bono consultant orientations, they are usually fired up and want to get on a project immediately. They can't wait.

That being said, on one of our earliest projects, we were having a hell of a time getting any of our largely Gen-X, pro bono marketing consultants to join a team. The project was to do branding and naming work for a critical organization serving low-income seniors in one of San Francisco's most challenged neighborhoods, the Tenderloin. When I pitched the project to our pro bono consultants, they begged for a different project. "I totally get that seniors are important, but I am 32, and it really isn't an issue that gets me excited," they shared. "Do you have anything focused on kids or the environment? I am really passionate about helping kids and the environment. That is our future." We shared with them the dire needs of the organization, and asked them to be open-minded and give it a try. If at the end they were unsatisfied, we would give them first dibs on the next round of projects. They reluctantly agreed.

Nine months later, I received a surprising email. The leader of the pro bono consulting team was urging me to attend a session at City Hall to protect funding for seniors in San Francisco. It turned out they had not only done a world-class job with the organization's brand; they had become an ongoing marketing committee for the organization, and several of them had become donors.

So many of us who are looking for a cause think we have to find our one true calling. We want to know that our mission is to help save one-legged kittens or find a cure for cancer. Hollywood stars helped popularize this notion with their high-profile focuses on particular issues, such as George Clooney (Darfur), Brad Pitt (New Orleans), Angelina Jolie (refugees), and Matt Damon (water). This is true of some of our elder statesmen too, like Al Gore (the environment) and President Jimmy Carter (Habitat for Humanity).

The idea of having a destiny is part of American mythology, and it applies to a lot more than social causes. It is our core mythology on just about every topic, from love to career: Who is my one true love? What am I going to be when I grow up?

I am also guilty of feeding into this way of thinking. When you are seeking resources or attention, being able to point to your success as part of your manifest destiny works incredibly well. People want to hear that you knew you were going to be a doctor/ basketball player/president/entrepreneur the minute you took your first step, still wearing diapers. Once you are successful, you are expected to tell a version of your biography that supports this mythology.

Destiny makes for a powerful story, but this concept is not only misleading, it does the next generation a great disservice, as it sets unrealistic and unhealthy expectations. Nearly all the early career professionals who seek an informational interview with me lament that they haven't found their cause yet. And while there are certainly people who are driven in this singular manner about a cause, it is almost always the result of a personal tragedy or an experience that inspired them to act. Maybe they were touched by the death of their mother from cancer, or their child died from gun violence. Still, this holds true only for a very small percentage of people, and it is by no means the only way to find purpose.

For the rest of us, seeking our purpose is about finding a direction, not a destination. That is, purpose is a verb, not a noun. We may never find one true calling, but we can understand the color of our purpose, which can help us have much more meaningful careers and lives.

TRUTH: Purpose isn't a cause; it is an approach to work and serving others. Purpose is a verb, not a noun.

Myth Two: Purpose = Luxury

Why do the poorest Americans donate 3.2 percent of their income to charity, compared to the wealthiest, who donate only 1.3 percent?[1] Why do people living in wealthier neighborhoods appear to be less generous?

Why also are those with the least money, education, and prestigious jobs more likely than their wealthy counterparts to say that they would keep their job even if they suddenly were financially set for life?[2] Why would a janitor continue to work if he won the lottery and an investment banker take an early retirement?

If you talk to people in lower prestige jobs and in poorer communities, they aren't surprised by these facts. They see it everyday and experience it firsthand. As a reverend in south central Los Angeles shared with me, "Being poor isn't so bad, it is just inconvenient." Purpose isn't a luxury only for those with money and security. Purpose is a universal need, and even those in challenging situations still make it a priority.

Arguably, the most famous advocate for purpose in history is Viktor Frankl, who wrote about the importance and presence of purpose in Nazi concentration camps, where he lived during the Holocaust. He found that purpose was key to his survival.

"Everything can be taken from a man but one thing: the last of human freedoms—to choose one's attitude in any given set of circumstances, to choose one's own way," Viktor famously wrote in *Man's Search for Meaning*.

It turns out that in many ways, the prioritization of purpose is inversely correlated with wealth. Money often conflicts with finding purpose, as it creates a false substitute for defining success.

TRUTH: Purpose is a universal need, not a luxury for those with financial wealth.

Myth Three: Purpose = Revelation

Connected to the myth that purpose is about a cause is the myth that we discover our purpose in one fell swoop. We are just walking along, minding our own business when—bam—our life's calling is transmitted to us like a bolt of lightning from above.

True, this is usually how superheroes find their purpose. Batman saw his parents murdered, and it became his purpose to fight crime in Gotham City. Superman discovered that his people were wiped out because of civil war and found his purpose in fostering peace and civility. But the reality is that this is not how it usually happens for us mere mortals.

"We don't receive wisdom; we must discover it for ourselves after a journey that no one can take for us or spare us," Marcel Proust famously observed.

Most of us will work for 45 to 50 years. Think about that for a second. That is the same amount of time it would take to attend college twelve times. And it's increasingly true that during that time, we will hold many different jobs, and for more and more of us, those will be in a range of fields. We have so many opportunities to find the work that best suits our perspective on the world and the way we most enjoy contributing.

TRUTH: Purpose is a journey. It doesn't come as a revelation from above, but from living life awake and seeking new experiences.

Myth Four: Only Some Work Generates Purpose

Administrative assistants spend their days supporting executives and have little autonomy or control over their workflow. Much of their work is repetitive and stressful, but it pays the bills and enables them to have the income they need to support the rest of their lives. It's just a job—a 9 to 5. Well, yes and no. It turns out that this is true, but only for about a third of administrative assistants, and perhaps more surprisingly, it is also true for about a third of every occupation.[3] What we do is not nearly as important as how we do it and what attitude we bring to the work. As the saying states, "Wherever you go, there you are." What we get from work has more to do with us than the work itself.

Work plays very different roles in people's lives. For some people, a job is simply a job. For them work is a paycheck, and they don't seek anything else from it. It enables them to have the money to enjoy their lives outside their job—they are not looking to derive meaning from their work. Those with careers care more deeply about their work as way to get ahead within their profession or function. It brings social status and power, which boosts their self-esteem.[4] Finally, those with callings fully integrate their work into their lives and values. They see work as integral to who they are and part of their lives.[5]

Amy Wrzesniewski and her colleagues found that across occupations, there were fairly even divides between people who saw their work as a job, career, or calling. It reinforced previous research that had demonstrated the ways individuals view work may be more tied to their psychological traits than to the work itself.[5]

Another study by Amy Wrzesniewski showed correlations between experiencing work as a calling and overall well-being and health.[6] This implies something very important: It is in your best interest to see work as a calling, and as a society, we need to shift more towards calling-based work.

Truth: You can find purpose in any job. It is all in how you approach it.

Myth Five: Purpose = Easy

Running a marathon hurts. There are the blisters, the chafing, and the body aches.

And yet, completing a marathon is something that many report as being incredibly meaningful. It pushes runners to their limits, both physically and emotionally.

Professional athletes make it look so easy. When we watch them, they appear natural and effortless. In reality, athletes work incredibly hard and endure tremendous pain to be successful. As fans, we rarely witness the injuries or watch the thousands of hours of monotonous practice. Winning the race or game is amazing, but their satisfaction stems from their deep investment.

With athletes, the relationship between pain and gain is clearest, but the same holds true of doing any work where we are experiencing high levels of purpose. Even when doing work that is making a big impact, if there is no skin in the game, the depth of purpose is diminished. As Viktor Frankl also said, "Man's main concern is not to gain pleasure or to avoid pain, but rather to see a meaning in his life."

As Jennifer Benz put it, "Purpose doesn't free you from working hard and being challenged, it will actually inspire and drive you to put yourself further out of your comfort zone. The falls will be harder, but the wins will feel so much better."

TRUTH: Purpose requires giving of yourself.

The Truth About Purpose

Purpose is for everyone, regardless of our profession or socioeconomic status. It is not about a cause or something that we discover by revelation. It is a challenging and rewarding journey.

6
The WHO, HOW & WHY of Purpose

Frank Santoni served for several years as the director of the Catholic Campus Ministry at Southern Methodist University. While he had his share of conversations with students about the day-to-day moral test associated with being an undergraduate student, his core counseling was for students struggling with the exploration of purpose in their life and careers after graduation.

This is the same conversation so many faculty members in every department of every university find themselves having with students. HR professionals today also face questions about purpose from employees all the time, and it is the subject of countless informational interview requests social entrepreneurs receive. It is also the driving force behind the amazing growth of the "life coaching" profession in the last ten years.

Frank left SMU to become the executive director of Dallas Social Venture Partners, a nonprofit network of wealthy and philanthropically-minded people in the region. In his new role, he finds himself having the same conversation he did back on campus. Despite great success and wealth, his members are hungry for conversations about personal purpose and impact.

The first edition of Richard Nelson Bolles's *What Color is Your Parachute?* was self-published in 1970. It has since sold over ten million copies around the world. It was a groundbreaking book for the Boomer generation. It popularized the idea that what you enjoy doing most is usually what you are best at doing. It was a revolutionary idea 40 years ago, but today is largely accepted in most circles.

But to Richard's question, I would add another: "What color is your purpose?" It is a critical question and one that we have yet to find common language around. We have language to talk about everything, from our education to our skills to strengths to our titles, but we don't have a shared way to talk about who we are and what matters to us personally.

Even employers are finding that old ways of describing our professional selves are not as effective as we once thought. Laszlo Bock, Google's SVP of HR, has found that "GPA and test scores are worthless as a hiring criteria."[1] In short, what we put on our resumés is largely not the stuff that matters.

In 1983, Harvard's Howard Gardner published his break-through theory of multiple intelligences. He laid out a framework for looking beyond traditional measures of IQ. A measure of some-one's intelligence is made up of seven distinct forms of intelligence: existential, naturalistic, intrapersonal, interpersonal, kinesthetic, mathematical, linguistic, spatial, and musical. IQ and GPA don't begin to measure all of these.

But what Gardner found twenty years later was that intelligence only mattered in the service of purpose. The key, his research revealed, was to have a highly articulated purpose.[2] His research took a major shift to focus on responsibility at work and how we bring our values into the office.

It is critical that you own your purpose and can articulate it powerfully as part of your identity. In working with thousands of professionals around the world and across sectors, patterns have emerged about how different people gain purpose in their work. Over the last 18 months, I have tested these patterns with leading researchers in the field and in workshops to validate what I was seeing at Taproot. The result is what we have come to call "purpose

Purpose Patterns

WHO you work to impact

WHY you do what you do

HOW you achieve that

WHO	WHY	HOW
· Individual	· Harmony	· Community-oriented
· Society	· Karma	· Structure-driven
· Organization		· Human-centered
		· Knowledge-driven

patterns"—a term coined by my colleague Phi-Hong Ha. It is an attempt to speak about purpose as a society within a standalone frame.

Want to discover your Purpose Pattern? Visit Imperative.com. A quick assessment will help you define where you generate purpose at work.

And when it comes to purpose at work, there are three core drivers that will determine whether we feel fulfilled in what we're doing: who we serve, how we serve them, and why we serve them. While we all generate purpose from a wide range of sources, people tend to have specific patterns in how they find purpose based on their own psychological profile.

When people would ask about this work, I first often described it as creating a Myers-Briggs or Strengths Finder for purpose. But as we researched purpose patterns, we came to realize that purpose is a somewhat different beast. Going beyond psychological analysis or personality inventories, creating your mission statement is about defining your true north and acting on it, making it personalized and in your own voice.

For over a decade, I have been working with nonprofits to develop their mission statements. For a nonprofit, their mission statement is their reason for being. It is their purpose. It guides their decisions, both big and small, and it serves as their bottom line. Similarly, a purpose pattern is most powerful when it is expressed in your own words and in a format akin to a mission statement.

To proactively infuse purpose into your work and life, clearly understanding what drives purpose for you greatly increases your odds of success. You need a mission, or better yet, a purpose statement, a short and powerful way to remember what matters and keep it front and center in your daily work. The purpose patterns that we've identified provide an outline and a starting place for us to each create our own personal purpose statement. It gives us the who, the how, and the why that we can then put into our own words and hang on our literal or figurative wall in the office.

My purpose is: *to work to create communities that are empowered to realize their potential.* The "who" are communities, which often take the form of organizations. It doesn't mean individuals or all of society, but rather groups of people who form a collective towards meeting a goal. The "how" is both in the acts of creating communities and empowering them. It is about creating the ecosystem that empowers people to do things they could never do on their own. Finally, the "why" for me is all about realizing potential. I get such a purpose boost when I see potential realized and not squandered. When a vision is achieved, it isn't only a victory for the people involved, but also is a win for everyone. It shows what we are capable of doing and fuels hope.

WHO of Purpose

My neighbor is an eye doctor. She sees patients every day. The vast majority of her patients suffer from a handful of common conditions, many a natural byproduct of old age. She helps people every day in a very tangible way. She loves it.

I, on the other hand, wouldn't last a week as a doctor. After seeing a couple of cases of glaucoma or cataracts, I would be ready to move on. Check—got it. What's next? It was part of why I found I wasn't meant to be a teacher—you never graduate. I am actually pretty extreme in this area, but my case is illustrative. Where some people see each person as unique and wonderful, I see patterns and have trouble focusing on each person as an autonomous individual. Some people have trouble seeing the forest through the trees. I tend to see the forest and not the trees.

The converse is also true. One of the most common sources of turnover at Taproot, with both team and board members, is the realization that we are too far removed from the front lines, and that they are meant to work directly with people and make an impact directly in their lives. Helping a nonprofit become stronger is intellectually satisfying but not engaging for them. We lose many talented pro bono consultants for the same reason—they want to be working directly with those in need.

My friend James Shepard once roughly described this as the difference between a doctor and a hospital administrator. Many people want to directly serve those in need, while others (like me) like to build the systems that enable and support doctors. For the latter, our playground is advancing organizations. We see organizations and groups of people as the organizing units of society.

My cousin, Jason Elliott, is a policy aid to the mayor of San Francisco. His work arena represents another type of playground. His passion is for working at a policy level, analyzing how city, state, and federal programs impact hospitals and clinics and can also set those places up better for success. He is about as far removed from the front lines as you can be, but the impact of even the smallest decision at that level can affect thousands of patients.

In my early twenties, I began to realize that my playground is organizations. I am intellectually curious about policy and broader changes in systems, but they tend to move too slowly to meet my need for experimentation and feedback. Changing policies and whole systems tends to take decades, and then years longer to see if they worked. This work is so removed from the front lines that it doesn't give me an emotional charge. I also enjoy working to help individuals sometimes, and working on the intersection of organizations and society. But at the core for me is a love for helping organizations realize their potential.

As you seek to have more purpose in your career, this is the first area where you should seek clarity. Are you a doctor, a hospital administrator, or policy-maker? This isn't an intellectual question; it has to do with what turns you on and ultimately, what will allow you to create the most meaningful impact in the world.

Individual: *Abigail Donahue*

Face-to-face with human potential, I feel my whole heart at work. These moments exemplify times when I've felt the deepest sense of purpose in my life. Working alongside my students, directly serving communities in need, feels meaningful and engaging in ways I can't fully articulate. I observe awareness and altruism accumulating in small acts of kindness. Someone who needs food is fed; someone who wants a chance to speak is heard. In these moments, I see a new world evolving right in front of me.

For me, individual transformation leads to social impact. Though nebulous social issues require vast structural shifts, I believe personal connection to these issues is what changes society. Beliefs, theories, policies, and laws need to change for social justice to occur; each person's actions drive these changes; and embodying these changes takes a personal commitment from everyone. I see my work as part of this social change feedback loop.

Organization: *Elaine Mason*

My role enables me to reach thousands of people, setting them up in the best way possible to achieve personal and professional success. My team recently finished working with a newly-formed business group, where we worked with the senior leadership team to redefine how their organization would produce and market new products. This was the first time the group worked this way, and the results of our work impacted every member of the organization.

At the close of the project, the group president hosted a town hall to explain the new way of working and the rationale behind all of the changes. During the town hall's open Q&A, many team members thanked her for thinking things through and making it easier for everyone to succeed in their group. One team member commented that it was the first time he ever experienced a leader that was so thoughtful. In response, the group president asked my team to come on stage and acknowledged that she hadn't worked that way in the past, but in partnership with my team, she saw the importance of defining meaning in everyone's role. Knowing that my team was able to improve the work life of so many people reminds me of how impactful my work can be across an organization.

Society: *Tera Pierce*

The laws of our land usually come from one person or group who experience a barrier in their life and bring it forward to a governing body, trying to change it for the next person. It is, in a way, a form of paying it forward. Generally, laws are not perfect the first time around and have unintended consequences. It is up to the legislature to listen to their constituents and amend our laws so that they can do what they are intended to do. Being involved in this kind of work is exciting, empowering, interesting, and constantly changing.

I love the work I do. As a trained social worker now working in public policy, I am able to facilitate changes to policies that have negative impacts on underserved and vulnerable populations, as well as craft new policies that will help break the cycle of poverty or addiction and expand access to education and vital services. It is fascinating work and changes daily. On a given day, I can be working on policy that stops predatory businesses from posting mugshots online, to mandating vision screenings for kids in school to prevent blindness and help them succeed.

WHY of Purpose

The foundation for our purpose is our moral view of the world. We are each driven in our work to drive progress toward achieving what we view as a moral utopia, where our values are universally achieved. It is our definition of progress, our motivation to move forward as a people.

Jonathan Haidt, a researcher at New York University, is the leader of a group of social and cultural psychologists who have been studying what they have dubbed moral foundations theory. They traced back our moral foundations to our earliest beginnings— first as apes, and then later as tribes. Their theory has now been tested around the world and helps to explain why morality varies so much by culture but retains many "similarities and recurrent themes." The theory is based on the ideas of anthropologist Richard Shweder, who defined six clusters of moral concerns: *care/harm*, *fairness/cheating*, *liberty/oppression*, *loyalty/betrayal*, *authority/subversion*, and *sanctity/degradation*.

What Jonathan and his team found was that these six foundations are the comprehensive lists from which political cultures and movements base their moral appeals.[3] Jonathan developed this theory through his lens as an expert in business ethics. He found that morality serves as the foundation for "intuitive ethics," which determines how we make decisions at work. It is always playing in the background as we operate in our work and in the larger world.

To simplify this framework, it is easiest to think of the moral foundations as they apply to work as being on a continuum between two moral poles. Like the notion of yin and yang, our society thrives when they are in balance. Neither is right or wrong, but rather critical ingredients to build a strong society. Even for those approaching the framework from a particular spiritual background, they likely will discover that what they believe to be the will of their god falls in line with one of these two poles.

The first pole Jonathan frames through the lens of karma. Karma is basically a moral version of Newton's laws of motion: for every action, there is an equal and opposite reaction. As Jonathan puts it, karma dictates that "kindness, honesty and hard work will (eventually) bring good fortune; cruelty, deceit and laziness will (eventually) bring suffering."[4]

He goes further and describes the belief in karma among those believe it to be as natural as gravity. It is a belief in how the world works. Nature will ensure in the long run that everyone gets his or her just desserts. It is our job to get out of the way and let karma work. This is a set of moral beliefs that value market forces. They trust the market and system to create a fair society, which ultimately delivers karma. It might not be immediate, but it will happen, and it will create the right carrots and sticks to optimize the results for the largest number of people.

The other pole doesn't trust that karma and nature will ensure that everyone gets what is coming to them. All around them, they see examples of injustice. They see natural forces as inhumane and brutal. Where those with a moral foundation based on karma might subscribe to a moral version of Newton's laws of motion, this other group sees natural forces as something more akin to entropy. They believe that without intervention, all groups and societies will move from order to disorder. It is only with intervention that we can be a moral society. They see harmony as the moral ideal and elevate it over competition.

An ideal world is one that erases boundaries between groups and people. We don't create success by pitting ourselves against each other, but by caring for others and building a society with room for everyone. This doesn't happen by itself. It requires constant social engineering and intervention. It is the moral responsibility of everyone to be vigilant to find where entropy is occurring and help return it to a sense of harmonious order. Harmony is based on empathy and compassion. It is based on seeing a moral society that is made up of individuals who need empathy and support to protect them from the chaos and injustice of nature.

We all sit somewhere in this continuum. It defines the underlying motivation behind our work. Within any job, we operate based on our assumptions about a moral society and take actions to advance our progress toward that utopic vision. Like most people, I am not on either extreme, but my core belief is that natural forces push us to entropy, and that human intervention is required. I see the primary role of organizations and society as managing that delicate balance between nature and humanity.

Karma: *David B. McGinty*

My life's purpose became more acutely focused on helping non-governmental organizations (NGOs), social enterprises, and inclusive and responsible businesses be more efficient change-makers and install the right incentives to achieve sustainable development outcomes.

For years, I've worked on building ecosystems of telecom-munication companies, funders, governments, and NGOs to create jobs and support families by delivering deep-field, mobile phone-based health care and education systems. Yesterday was spent working through alternative models for pub-lic-private partnerships to provide emergency transportation for expecting mothers in remote areas. This afternoon, my team is building a mezzanine of philanthropic and commercial invest-ments to drive economic growth that incorporates smallholder farmers. Tomorrow, we are helping a NGO redesign its internal business processes to more efficiently support external cross-sector collaboration. Next week, we are looking at expansion plans to provide youth support services in sub-Saharan Africa.

Harmony: *Bentley Davis*

When I ran the free clinic, we also had a dental clinic. We had a part-time hygienist who took care of cleanings and preventative care, but treatment was harder to find. The longest wait was for dentures. When explaining poverty to someone who thinks that one can just pull themselves up from their bootstraps, I always use the example of those missing teeth. It is very hard to get any job, even a low-paying job, if one is missing front teeth. In the course of my travels, I met a denturist and explained the need. She volunteered to do a set of dentures per month for free. My first patient to get dentures was a working-age woman who had been waiting for over a year. She couldn't find work and had been embarrassed to smile. After she got her dentures, she was elated. I still have the thank-you note she sent me.

HOW of Purpose

Even with the same moral foundations defining success, we approach the process of getting there differently. How we work is also tied to our view of the world and how we both solve problems and engage in the creative process. We can perhaps gain the most purpose in our work in how we approach it. Insight into how we approach work emerged while doing research on promising solutions to strengthen K–12 education in the United States. As I dug in, I found incredibly diverse assessments and solutions.

The more I listened, what emerged was that people had fundamentally diverse thinking styles. These styles profoundly influenced how they engaged in addressing the opportunity to improve education in the country, as illustrated in the following examples.

Community-Centered

If you look at the best schools in the country, you find one thing they all have in common: incredible parent participation and leadership. The parents are well-informed and invested in the school's success, and they hold the school accountable for results; they also find ways to generate resources and advocate for the school within the community. To improve education in this country, we must learn why some schools have this kind of parent involvement and build that capacity. You can never know what challenges a school will face in the future, but with strong parent and community involvement, schools can face any challenge.

Human-Centered

Have you been in a typical public school classroom lately, especially in a big city? How do we expect a child to be inspired and learn in that kind of environment? The school is more like a prison than a place to promote feelings of well-being that help students learn and focus. We need to build pupil-based schools that provide fresh air and light. They need enough space for students to work without banging into each other, and classrooms need to be arranged to create natural social settings that encourage communication. If we want kids focused, they also need healthy food. And why are we asking teenagers to come to school at the break of dawn, when all the research says this isn't natural and makes learning nearly impossible?

Structure-Driven

We don't provide the right training, support, or tools to teachers and principals. We need to design effective leadership practices, policies, and procedures for school systems. We need to redesign curriculum and pedagogy (i.e., educational approach) that works with the needs of today's kids, and help teachers adopt the new design so they can be set up for success. With this kind of support, our principals and teachers can achieve anything.

Knowledge-Driven

Improving education requires that we look at the data and research and build upon it. We don't know what successful education even means today; we are blindly just continuing to use old models that don't work anymore. We don't know enough about education and what success looks like for today's schools. We continue to take the test and fail, because we ourselves aren't doing our homework.

In my experience, all of these mindsets are true, and yet not one of them would provide the level of change we need to see in our educational system. The point here isn't about being right, but rather understanding each perspective about how the world works. There is a tremendous need for all these approaches. It's my experience that people will find that their sense of purpose and engagement directly ties to their ability to work in alignment with their perspective about the best ways to further change.

These perspectives are not confined to education or even nonprofits. We see them in how people approach challenges and opportunities in just about any setting. Some people are always looking for ways to bring other people into an issue to help build ownership, community, and awareness. Some people see every situation as an opportunity to redesign it in order to better serve needs. Some people are laser focused on learning and understanding everything about an issue before they move forward. Others look for potential efficiency gains in every line they wait in, and know there is a better way to design processes to bring out the best in people and keep their time focused on the things that matter.

Community-Centered: *Jennifer King*

For me, it's about facilitating connections that lead to social impact. Connections between philanthropists and social change organizations. Between photographers and social cause projects. Between business and nonprofits. It seems to be the common theme to the moments I feel purpose most strongly. One moment where I felt purpose in my work related to community social impact was the day of the Venture4Change summit, a one-day event I developed that brought together businesses, social ventures, funders, community leaders, and nonprofits. It was an opportunity to find common ground, talk about mutual challenges and opportunities, and break down silos and build bridges. I felt tremendous satisfaction to see more than 100 people from all backgrounds engaged in deep and meaningful discussion about our community and how we can work together to drive social change.

Human-Centered: *Rebekah Heppner*

I had the opportunity to serve as interim CEO at a nonprofit organization during a period of transition. This was a very difficult time for the people who worked there, being surrounded by uncertainty about the future and not knowing who the next leader would be or what changes he or she would make. In addition to keeping up with the day-to-day work of the organization, I was able to get to know the staff members individually and provide them with a sense of stability. We were able to keep the lines of communication open between staff and the board, which made both the individuals and the organization stronger. When I left after six months, the staff not only threw me a party, but each person handed me a rose with a note attached, expressing what my time in the organization had meant to them.

I try to select projects and plan activities that allow me to meet individually with people. In my work as an applied anthropologist, I primarily conduct interviews to learn a person's individual viewpoint about a situation or experience, then synthesize the information to find common themes. For example, my dissertation research, which has recently been published as a book, contained career-history interviews of former women executives who, like me, have left their corporate careers behind and found more meaningful work. I analyzed those interviews to find themes, and the book is built around stories the women told me, providing a glimpse of the culture that exists in the contemporary corporation.

Structure-Driven: *Stephanie Fuentes*

Because of the influence of data (or a lack of it), I regularly offer to facilitate meetings and brainstorming sessions in decision-making and to help focus the discussion. I look for ways to apply logic models to my projects and help others with theirs. And I don't give up. This work takes a long time to bring to fruition, so I have to be able to see the unseen potential in the situation in order to shepherd my clients through the journey. I often have to work knowing people may not see the integration of the system I can see until they reach the very end. As an example, in the past 18 months in my current position, I've redesigned and re-launched over ten major evaluation and data collection projects for the organization. Some results have led to strategic shifts in communication for the organization and a better focus on business results. Most importantly, people are now talking about what data they have or can get that will help them decide what to do.

I absolutely love the process of asking questions of my client (external or internal) and watching the process unfold as they discover for themselves what is important, what is meaningful, and how to measure it. I never know how it will turn out until the model is complete. It's a co-creation through structured conversation. If I could do logic models every day, I would—they are the epitome of fun.

Knowledge-Driven: *Daniel Reif*

I'm generally asked to look at data for two reasons: to answer a question about it, or to figure out a way to better manage it (capturing it, storing it, moving it, or presenting it). To do so, I'll begin by understanding the applications, people, or processes that create the data I'm interested in. Once I've captured all of the factors that create the data, I'll use SAS to model how events or changes to the process will impact it. What is unique about this is that it makes apparent how well or how poorly you understand the data you are analyzing. If an event occurs, and you can exactly explain why and how it changed the data you are analyzing, there is a definitiveness to the knowledge that you've gained, which I think is hard to come by when not dealing with numbers. This has given me the confidence that I fully understand complex problems, as well as the ability to clearly use data to explain them to others, something I find very rewarding. As I move from one project or subject to another, I feel that I'm amassing more and more knowledge and making progress toward understanding the health care industry. This gives me a strong sense of purpose.

To infuse purpose proactively into your work and life, clearly understanding what drives purpose for you greatly increases your odds of success. You need a mission, or better yet, a purpose statement. You need a short and powerful way to remember what matters.

7
The Practice of Purpose

"You can't escape the responsibility of tomorrow by evading it today."—Abraham Lincoln

Jennifer McCrea, or J-Mac as she is better known, teaches at Harvard and works with many of the top social entrepreneurs in the world as a fundraising consultant. She founded a course on exponential fundraising, and it is wildly popular. In being a practitioner and teacher for years, she has come to believe that the two keys to success in fundraising are seeing the world as full of ample resources, and viewing fundraising as relationships rather than transactions.

These two insights are also at the core of practicing purpose at work. Purpose is around us in great abundance. If we approach work seeing purpose as scarce, we are likely to manifest a self-fulfilling prophecy. Similarly, if we see work as a transaction and series of tasks rather than being about relationships and practicing our art, we will never be able to look up from our screen to embrace the purpose all around us. Jennifer has found that the key to building fundraising relationships is connecting with people through shared purpose. Again, it isn't necessarily about a cause, but often rather more mundane, day-to-day moments of purpose. This connection is personal and intimate. It is about relating as humans and celebrating what matters in our lives.

After years of practicing her art at work, Jennifer now uses it at home with her young children. When she isn't on the road and can be home for dinner, she has her family reflect on the purpose they experienced in their day. When her kids leave the nest, she wants to be sure they are purpose-literate and are in awe of the world around them. In her simple exercise, she asks everyone at the table to reflect on what surprised, inspired, and moved them during the day. She calls this SIM (surprised, inspired, and moved). It brings out the sun on even the rainiest of days.

If people do nothing else everyday to practice purpose, doing SIM on their commute home will radically increase their odds of finding the next day rich in purpose. It is a daily two-minute meditation that can allow everyone to discover purpose. It focuses you on the present, and studies show that those that live in the present are happier than those that focus on the past or future.[1]

Meaning-Making

Each semester, when Amy Wrzesniewski at Yale's School of Management begins her course on careers, she shares a simple fact that is profoundly upsetting to her students: The average graduate of their program will work for three different organizations within their first five years out of the MBA program. Many of them came to business school to find direction, and to hear that the journey continues so unsteadily after school is disappointing. They hoped they would leave school with it all figured out, but alas—no such luck.

This phenomenon is partly due to the nature of how we learn about ourselves and need to shuffle between jobs to gain experience. It is also largely a reality of the new nature of work, which has everyone looking more like a freelancer than a lifer. As Reid Hoffman writes in *The Start-Up of You*, we are increasingly thinking of our careers more entrepreneurially and see ourselves as start-ups, selling our time, talent, and networks.[2]

This approach creates a tremendous amount of freedom. We are not tied to one job or employer; we are the masters of our own destiny. But as Barry Schwartz observed, "On the other side of liberation sits chaos and paralysis."

This is what researchers Susan Ashford and Ruth Blatt at the University of Michigan wanted to explore. How do freelancers and others working outside a traditional work setting manage themselves? How do they monitor their time and stay disciplined? The answer would not only provide insight into this growing class of freelancers, but also give insights in how work is changing in the new "start-up of you" reality. To answer these questions, they interviewed dozens of professionals, from engineers to designers, who worked outside organizations. The motivations were pretty clear and consistent. As one writer shared with them, "The reason I wanted to be self-employed was I wanted this to be my life, no matter how much hard work it took to make sure that I was going to do what I wanted to do. I would rather go through the pain and suffering to make it work my way as opposed to riding the easy ride working for somebody nine to five." That is, they wanted the freedom to own their work.

But this kind of work does not come without its challenges. The people they interviewed also felt the onus of too much freedom. "Because the work environment is very much under my own control, it also means it's under my lack of control. So if I'm not on top of it, it can easily slide away." And the income can be unpredictable and unstable. "When I have a lot of work to do, I can't keep up, but then there are long stretches when I don't have any work to do. So it's hard to build up anything stable financially."

Professionals inside organizations share these challenges, but to a lesser degree. They are not living project-to-project, but often year-to-year, with potential gaps between gigs, and it generates many of the same symptoms. Many areas where challenges significantly overlap between people working inside and outside an organization involves the work itself. Sometimes we just don't like some of the tasks in our jobs, somewhat like an artist having to not just create, but also sell their work. We at times find ourselves doing work we aren't sure we believe in.

For example, the researchers spoke with a graphic designer working on a book design for a logging company. At a certain point, he realized, "They think raping and pillaging is good... You're just like, 'I can't believe I'm typesetting this, I can't believe I'm designing this so that it will look attractive.'"

Susan and Ruth began their research looking at how people set goals and manage their time when they are self-employed. But as they talked to people, they found that the key issues raised by everyone weren't about time or goal management; what everyone wanted to talk about was how to manage purpose. That was their primary concern. How do I stay motivated and engaged? How do I feel like my work matters? When things get tough, how do I stick it out?

These professionals were actively finding ways to make meaning for themselves and to endure their moments of pain. They were creating meaning, constructing a coherent narrative that linked their activities to a higher purpose and gave them significance.[3]

The prerequisite to effectively creating meaning was self-awareness. As one consultant shared with them, "I would suggest that the most important thing they could do was to really know themselves, to really understand how they think, what their mental models are, what they believe in, what they care about, how they show up in the world, what they project onto other people, what their shadow is, and to really, really know what this instrument is, and how it works." Or, as another subject shared, "I think the first thing I would do is figure out what your values are, and what you want to accomplish in life. Become clear on your own self-motivators, and you know, your intrinsic motivators."

Understanding the drivers of purpose in your work is foundational to managing that same purpose. If you don't have basic self-awareness of purpose, it is difficult to know how to productively create the narratives and practices that will work. You need to know the WHO, HOW, and WHY of what generates purpose for you.

In talking to these professionals, Susan and Ruth found that they had implemented four different ways to make meaning for themselves. These become key to practicing purpose and keeping it front and center. With each, professionals create purpose resources, stories, and actions that they use to either keep themselves out of the purpose void or work their way out of it.

The first is task-focused purpose. It means loving the craft of your work and overcoming small, task-related challenges. One database architect described how he works to optimize purpose in his tasks by broadening his contribution. As he described, "A large majority of what I do is understanding the business, understanding how it runs, and understanding not only how it runs now, but what it is that the customer would be interested in in the future."

Rather than just taking a task at face value, he would widen the scope to connect it to a broader task that required him to learn about its context and challenge his thinking. It not only provided the narrative he needed to understand why the work mattered, but also turned the task into a learning and growth opportunity.

Those using the second approach were impact-focused and created ways to see their work as having an impact on others, part of something bigger than themselves. They considered the impact on society, other people, and organizations. How was the work they were doing helping someone or the organization? What were the consequences of it not happening? Who would benefit from it downstream?

Those in the third approach focused on their own identity. How did they develop a sense of who they are and where they were going? Faced with the challenge of making sales calls and not feeling good about it, one professional shared that he created a narrative about who he wouldn't approach for work. "I would never work for a defense company, even though it may be a big contractor." In defining different aspects of their jobs and boundaries, these professionals were able to gain a better sense of themselves and their values. It also gave them a sense of integrity and power to know that they weren't just looking for any client.

Finally, the researchers tied it all back to financial drivers of purpose. While money itself is not a purpose, often the reason we need the money is important and purpose-driven. As one person shared, "To me, I look at my family and decide I have to do it." They see money as a means to enable them to achieve their most important purpose-based work—being part of a family. It is about survival and the ability to meet commitments.

Job Crafting

Most job descriptions are oriented around tasks and responsibilities, but it is rare to find "caring" on the list of responsibilities. Of course, there are exceptions like teachers, counselors and nurses, but it's not usually explicitly stated that we expect people to care for their colleagues, clients, or other people they engage with at work. Caring is often the difference maker, but it is largely invisible and unrecognized. In most cases, organizations see caring as outside their cultural definition of real work. It is seen as soft and not core to success. Worse yet, caring is viewed as inappropriate in the workplace. Companies create an environment where employees are not given the discretion or tools to exercise caring.

Amy Wrzesniewski, Jane Dutton, and Gelaye Debebe were particularly interested in this phenomenon when it came to what are known as "dirty" jobs, jobs that require physically or morally undesirable lines to be crossed. These jobs are viewed by others as onerous and odious by the employees or others.[4]

People working in dirty jobs are seen to have a hard time interacting with others, given the stigma of their work. Caring for others means engaging with others, and for many doing dirty work, they are expected to be nearly invisible within an organization.

This doesn't just apply to sanitation workers or morticians. It also applies to roles like working in a call center. I met with a member of the management team of a major telecommunications company, who openly talked about how the company views their call center employees as "sub-human."

In this case, the researchers were interested in the maintenance staff at a hospital, the folks who clean up after the sick, dying, and recently deceased. It is a dirty job, but in the context of a high-caring enterprise. How did these professionals find purpose in their work, and did they find themselves involved in the culture of caring for the hospital, or did they feel like invisible outsiders? Research confirmed that these patient room cleaners are treated with disrespect, and medical staff devalues their work. The cleaners reported feeling invisible to nurses and doctors. Even if they were in the same room, medical staff would rather call the cleaners' supervisor than speak with them directly. One staff member shared that "the doctors have a tendency to look at us like we're not even there, like, you know, we'll be working in the hallways, and you know, no recognition of what you are doing whatsoever."

Doctors and nurses will also do things to try to push their responsibility to the cleaners or make their job harder. Doctors, for example, would regularly drop their gloves on the floor after doing an exam rather than disposing of them. Others complained of nurses avoiding cleaning up bodily fluids and just dumping them on the floor so they became the responsibility of the cleaning team.

But the researchers also found that despite being undermined in every direction and being treated as sub-human, many of these cleaning professionals find ways to care for patients and find purpose in their work. Much of it is in their core work, keeping the hospital clean so that it is safe for those being treated. They see doing this work as elemental to taking care of the patients. But it doesn't stop there. The cleaners go out of their way to care for patients and even doctors and nurses. This is well outside their job descriptions, but for many it was what they described as the main driver of purpose in their work.

The majority of cleaners expressed genuine concern for patients and their families. They act on it different ways. Often, they will simply respond to requests from patients to retrieve things or take on small tasks that the patients' medical condition prevented them from doing. They will often fetch a nurse at a patient's request. Often, this work comes at the risk of being reprimanded by their supervisor. If a patient is lost, they will walk them where they need to go, even if it means disobeying strict orders not to leave their area. They put the needs of the patients over those of their manager.

One of the other ways they provide care is simply by talking to lonely patients. "A lot of times they want to hold a conversation with you. You know, they're lonely or sick already. I try to hold a conversation." Or they will engage in conversation with the family of a patient. "I talk with kids' parents quite a bit, you know, sometimes they'll mention what's wrong with their kids, you know. They just kind of want to talk." Many of the cleaners also shared stories of trying to entertain patients. They will dance to a song that is playing or try to make people laugh. Sometimes they do something more subtle, like changing the decorations in a room for someone in long-term care.

None of this is part of their job description, and in many cases can be frowned upon. They weren't simply doing the job and clocking out—they were taking ownership of their work and finding ways to craft their job to make it meaningful for them. They had changed their relationship with others to be able to provide care and, in the process, incorporate new tasks. They had redesigned their jobs to suit them rather than be a victim of its constraints.

Job crafting is a conscious or unconscious process of redesigning your own job to better align with your values, strengths, and passions.[5]

It is a relatively new area of study that is part of the broader, nascent field of positive psychology. As is clear from these stories of hospital workers, what researchers have found that much of what brings meaning to a job is not the job itself, but what we bring to it. In observing professionals in some of the toughest environments, such as the cleaning people, they are uncovering the natural ways people adapt to bring meaning to their work.

Traditional thinking says that the best way to find more meaningful work is to find a new job. But the theory behind job crafting points to another solution—changing the job you're in to better meet your needs. Positive psychologists have gone from observing organic job crafting, to documenting the process, to proactively facilitating job crafting. The results are remarkable and point to the fact that we have a lot more control over purpose at work than we may realize. Within job crafting, professionals can redesign not only their mindset, but also their tasks and relationships, as we saw with the cleaners. It is a process that anyone can use to boost purpose at work. And the best part is that applies to any role—from hospital administrator to maintenance worker.

Task crafting is about redesigning the tasks in a job. It can be about taking on more or fewer tasks, and it can also involve changing the approach or scope of a task. One of the most successful examples of this in my own work was in adding writing to my responsibilities. I made time on my commute to write blogs and articles, which gave me a creative outlet. It wasn't required of my job, but it added a lot of depth to my work, and also allowed me to explore issues that weren't part of my day-to-day.

Relational crafting involves changing your relationships with co-workers, clients, and others in your work environment. It is usually about changing the nature or depth of relationships. This can involve even simple changes, like taking someone to lunch once a week, or trying to have more meetings in person, rather than over email or the phone.

The final form of job crafting is cognitive crafting. It is much like what we explored with the freelancers who changed the way they thought about their work. They connected each thing they were doing with its purpose. It is about remembering why you are cleaning the room, conducting an audit, or designing a website.

Done well, this process stems from the WHO, HOW, and WHY of what drives purpose. Once you have that self-awareness, it is possible to intentionally redesign your job to make it substantially more rewarding. It can move you from being on the verge of quitting to finding the same job rich in purpose.

Resilience (When Enough Is Enough)

The two responses to danger are fight or flight. When faced with adversity at work, we tend to focus on either changing the situation or running away and finding a different job. Job crafting gives us powerful tools to fight back and turn it around. It enables us to take control of a situation that at first might feel helpless. Being resilient and resourceful is usually the best path—we can't spend our lives running and the costs associated with it can be incredibly high. Fleeing is usually the higher risk path.

But, there are times when job crafting and meaning-making don't cut it. There are times when it is important to make a bigger change to a new profession or a new employer. There are situations that are likely beyond crafting, or where the opportunity elsewhere is markedly better than anything that could be crafted. To maximize purpose, there are three reasons to jump ship (other than money).

The cliché, backed by research, is that most people take a job for the organization and leave because of their manager. No manager is perfect, but there are managers who are simply not a good fit for someone, or worse yet, are incompetent and undermining the teamwork of those around them. It may be possible to find a new manager inside an organization, but if someone is locked into a bad fit, it may require jumping ship.

Another reason to leave is the organization itself. If the values of the organization do not align with an employee, it is rarely something that can be fixed— -it becomes an issue of integrity. Working for an organization that does things an employee considers against their values overwhelms any purpose that could be gained by job crafting.

Finally, someone can find that they are in the wrong profession given their purpose drivers. If someone gains purpose from working on policy issues at a societal level, working with individuals as a teacher or doctor without the opportunity to impact larger scale change might feel too limiting. At times, it is better to flee than fight. Or, as President Kennedy said, "Efforts and courage are not enough without purpose and direction."

SECTION THREE
SOCIAL PURPOSE—THE PURPOSE ECONOMY ORGANIZATION

8
The Purpose Economy Organization

If you were online in 1997, there was about an 80 percent chance you were surfing the web using Netscape's browser. By 2002, Microsoft's Internet Explorer had secured 90 percent of the browser market. In its death throes, Netscape was purchased by AOL and eventually put to rest when AOL merged with TimeWarner. But by July 2013, Internet Explorer enjoyed only a 4 percent market advantage over Firefox, a new browser that rose from the ashes of Netscape.

It is a classic story of the Information Economy—the browser wars. Hidden in the story, however, is the remarkable story of a Purpose Economy organization and its inspiring success against Microsoft, the Goliath of the day. Microsoft had invested so many resources in Internet Explorer that by 1998, Netscape realized it could no longer compete. It had to shift its business model to be solvent, but it believed in the vision of the Netscape browser as being the "web for everyone," and as a critical platform to limit the power of Microsoft and its monopoly.

In 1998, Netscape decided to release the code of its browser to the public—to make it open source. If the company couldn't compete with Microsoft with money, perhaps someone else could find another way to compete. They called it the Mozilla open source project.

Within the first year, new community members from around the world had already contributed new functionality, enhanced existing features, and even become engaged in the management and planning of the project itself. By creating an open community, the Mozilla project had become larger than any one company.

In 2003, AOL and Mitch Kapor funded the launch of the Mozilla Foundation, a nonprofit that supported the work of this open source community. The Mozilla Foundation existed to ensure that the Internet would never become solely owned by companies. They had a profound sense of purpose—Internet for the people, by the people. The Mozilla Foundation was a movement first and an organization second.

And it wasn't even a single organization. Eventually, a commercial enterprise was formed within the nonprofit entity, establishing a hybrid organization to best serve the Mozilla community. The combined organizations grew to have hundreds of staff and over $100 million a year in revenue, but they only existed to serve the volunteers and users who believed in a web for everyone. This band of volunteers, as a nonprofit, achieved their goal of bringing down Microsoft's monopoly. They were able to do what the Netscape executives couldn't. In a truly remarkable effort, they proved that purpose and human capital could build a great business.

The Mozilla community is served by a nonprofit organization with a commercial enterprise embedded within it. It has a clear and powerful purpose and enables the fulfillment of purpose for its members. It embraces empowering coaching over controlling management. It strives to be transparent and have community engagement in decision-making. It doesn't draw a strong line between employees and other members of its community, nor does it use financial results as its primary measure of success. This recipe enabled it to achieve a level of success beyond the reach of Netscape, its Information Economy predecessor.

All of these factors comprise what makes the Mozilla Foundation such a powerful example of how organizations will thrive in the Purpose Economy. But as I explore throughout the following chapters, that isn't the only takeaway. There is a lot more to learn if you look more closely at how Mozilla operates today. In having to support thousands of volunteers on a seemingly impossible mission, Mozilla has developed a set of unique practices that are illustrative of a successful Purpose Economy organization.

The Purpose Economy Organization—Defined

Having a purpose or value proposition doesn't necessarily make a Purpose Economy organization. Monsanto, one of the most destructive companies on the planet, has a purpose. Altria, the king of tobacco, would argue they have a purpose. McDonald's has a purpose. Chevron has a purpose.

Every organization has a purpose or value proposition, or it quickly dies. A Purpose Economy organization creates purpose for its employees and customers—through serving real needs, enabling personal growth, and building community.

It is perhaps misleading to talk about a Purpose Economy organization as a binary label. There is no organization that you would say is 100 percent a Purpose Economy organization, just as there is no building that is 100 percent sustainable. It is a matter of degrees.

Take Google, for example. Larry Page and Sergey Brin founded Google with a strong commitment to creating purpose for people. Their products have improved countless lives by helping us access critical information when we need it, and their management remains deeply committed to creating positive social impact. At the same time, the rapid growth of the company has left many of its employees hungry for purpose. Furthermore, the same technology that is improving lives is also being used to sell ads to companies pitching products that are destructive to people and the world.

Conversely, Walmart has been part of the most destructive trends of the last 50 years. Its negative impact on local business, community, and labor has been well-documented. At the same time, the company is at the heart of massive changes to move consumer product companies to create more sustainable products and inclusive supply chains.

Are Google and Walmart Purpose Economy organizations? Like humans, organizations are complicated and full of tensions and challenges. Even the most successful organizations, those who are focused on creating purpose for people, have their challenges. A Purpose Economy organization is one that makes the creation of purpose their imperative, even if they struggle at times to realize their values and vision.

Three Core Approaches

Purpose Economy organizations are emerging with incredibly diverse ways to emphasize purpose. Organizations that are thriving in the new economy integrate at least one of these three methods into their enterprise: 1) delivering purpose to customers, consumers, or participants, 2) providing purpose to employees, and/or 3) building purpose throughout the supply chain.

Harvard MBA Will Dean founded Tough Mudder and has built a rapidly growing business out of extreme obstacle courses "designed to test your all-around strength, stamina, mental grit, and camaraderie." These courses push people to face their fears as they make their way through mud, fire, ice water, and 10,000 volts of electricity. Over a million people around the globe have participated in these obstacle courses and have found the experience of training and participating to be one of powerful personal growth.

Tough Mudder was intentionally designed not as a race, but as a team challenge. People typically sign up with friends and support each other throughout the training and the actual event. It is part of the Tough Mudder pledge to "put teamwork and camaraderie before course time." This makes the process social, and in making the success of their peers part of their goal, the participants, or

"Mudders," gain a sense of service. In so doing, Tough Mudder provides Mudders with personal and social purpose.

Tough Mudder delivers purpose. That is their service. Creating purpose is their value proposition to their customers. This is the first approach to a Purpose Economy organization.

The second approach focuses on providing purpose to employees. Avon has been doing this for more than 125 years. It was inspired less by the needs of customers and more by a vision to make direct sales relevant to women. Avon's purpose has been to create "a means for women to earn their own money at a time when not many women worked outside the home." Furthermore, at the time of its founding, "it connected women, who were otherwise isolated." Avon was critical to building female independence in the economy and giving women a source of purpose. It has come a long way since then but has retained its core vision of empowering women through work.

The tea company Guayaki Yerba Mate is a compelling example of the third approach to purpose. They are building purpose through their supply chain—those people and companies that provide them with tea. The company's core goal is to create 1,000 jobs and restore 200,000 acres of rainforest by 2020. They have built a network of certified Fair Trade tea growers that have created jobs for indigenous people in Argentina, Paraguay, and Brazil.

The company's growth goals are tied to their purpose. They know that to make their desired impact, they must grow 25 percent every year until 2020. It is a daunting goal, but with purpose in their sails, they have stayed on track since they began in 1996. Their efforts increase purpose not just within the limits of the company, but in every person that contributes to the overall business in some fashion.

Purpose as DNA

Attending a barbecue as a 12-year-old, Josie Maran was asked by a woman if she wanted to be in a fashion show. An agent saw her in the show and encouraged her to go professional. She did, and several years later, she starred in a Backstreet Boys video.

Josie went from being a model to a supermodel. For three consecutive years, she was in the *Sports Illustrated* swimsuit issue, and she booked gigs for many top brands, from Victoria's Secret to Guess. Finally, Josie was named the spokesmodel for Maybelline: "Maybe she's born with it. Maybe it's Maybelline." She herself had become a global brand.

But Josie realized this wasn't enough. As she shared with me, "I need meaning in my life as much as I need air," and selling Maybelline was leaving her short of breath. She realized that she had the opportunity to stop peddling unhealthy body images and often-toxic makeup to women and girls. As a supermodel, she now had the ability to create a cosmetics company that aligned with her values.

In 2007, she launched Josie Maran Cosmetics, a line of natural cosmetics committed to the protection and improvement of nature and the environment. Using her status in the industry, Josie quickly got deals with QVC and Sephora and became a force in the industry.

Josie Maran Cosmetics has seen wild financial success, but it has also helped create changes in the industry. Josie has built demand for natural cosmetics and inspired her competition to change their lines and create new ones.

Her success in the emerging Purpose Economy wasn't just due to the sense of purpose that her products provided to customers. It was in how she built, led, and continues to lead the company. When Josie started the company, it was vital to build "a sense of purpose into its DNA." She remains "100 percent convinced that a big part of Josie Maran Cosmetics' success is that everyone is encouraged to bring their whole selves to work, and we're unified by our passion for taking care of the world as one way to take care of our company and ourselves."

Josie integrated all three purpose approaches into her company. She enabled her customers to gain purpose by caring for themselves and the planet. She created a work culture that celebrated work and seeks to maximize purpose for everyone on the team. Finally, she has invested in creating a supply chain for her company that supports women in Morocco. Purpose is fully part of the company's DNA.

Josie, like other leaders in the new economy, understands the incredible power of purpose in business. As Courtney Hall, former captain of the NFL's San Diego Chargers and managing director for Hillcrest Venture Partners, told me, "Purpose is the Holy Grail for organizations." It is the currency of the new economy, and Courtney, like other venture capitalists, is seeing that those organizations "that understand and create purpose will be the leaders of the next economic era."

Transitional Approaches

Other companies see the need for purpose, but know that they can't just make a radical change and drop all their existing services. Companies like Pepsi aren't going to just stop making unhealthy drinks and snacks altogether, but they know they need to find ways to begin changing and to signal this intent to their employees and customers.

For many companies, cause-based marketing has emerged as a popular way to infuse their products with purpose. Typically, they are partnering with nonprofit organizations and then drafting off of their purpose. For example, luxury brand Gucci marketed its bags in 2013 by committing to donate 25 percent of the retail price to benefit UNICEF's support of schools in Asia and Africa. The bags don't inherently provide purpose, but bundling the bag with services for the poor adds perceived purpose to the purchase.

Hundreds of companies are following suit, and nonprofit organizations are enjoying a new revenue stream. Cause-based marketing has built awareness for key issues in the world and generated needed funds for nonprofit organizations. It is working as a transitional strategy as companies make deeper changes. 93 percent of Millennials and 92 percent of mothers said they would switch brands if the company was involved in a good cause and the price was the same.[1]

But as we explored in Section Two, purpose and cause are not the same thing, and donating to a cause doesn't change the fundamental nature of their products and services. Cause-based marketing helps to begin to turn the ship, but it will hopefully prove to be a transitional strategy rather than a permanent one.

Similarly, many companies see the need to provide more purpose for their employees but can't risk making a radical switch. It's impossible to change the culture of a huge company like Bank of America or Hewlett-Packard overnight. Companies still need to attract and retain top talent and find a way to make a down payment on the change.

Companies are making the incremental change by turning to employee volunteerism and charitable giving programs. Like cause-based marketing, these programs don't change the nature of the company's core, but bundle a meaning into the existing experience to make it more desirable. Like cause-based marketing, it also appears to be working. Millennials who frequently participate in their company's volunteer activities are twice as likely to rate their corporate culture as very positive, as compared to Millennials who rarely or never volunteer.[2]

New organizations have emerged to help companies build and manage these programs. One of the most successful to date has been Causecast, founded by Ryan Scott. He made his first fortune as the co-founder of NetCreations, an email communications platform, and is now well on his way to make a fortune again. Founded in 2007, Causecast is already profitable and includes some of the largest companies in the United States among its clients.

Causecast has built a platform that enables company employees to do everything from volunteering, to donations, to leading cause campaigns. Where information is the currency of the current economy, Ryan believes that "purpose is the currency of the new economy." Ryan has successfully transitioned from a visionary in the Information Economy to one in the new economy. He sees that "capitalism, if applied creatively, holds the potential to transform the complex social, economic, and environmental challenges facing the world today."

In the next three chapters, I explore how an organization can thrive in the new economy. Chapter 9 scans key industries, how they are changing, and key opportunities to create value. The following chapter provides an overview of how the needs of employees are changing and the ways in which organizations need to adjust to address them. The final chapter in this section examines the new skills needed to lead and manage an organization.

9
Purposeful Ventures—Five Opportunities

While the Information Economy has created many marvelous inventions and improvements in our society, one of the unfortunate side effects has been a loss of connection in many parts of our lives. In her book *Alone Together: Why We Expect More from Technology and Less from Each Other,* MIT professor Sherry Turkle illustrates the irony that even as people are spending so much time on social media sites, they're finding less authentic connection and more isolation[1]

But the Purpose Economy promises something different. Technology now has the potential to connect us in more authentic, meaningful ways, rather than isolating us, and we have come to need this connection more and more. This shift in the use of technology is enabling radical changes to markets and organizations. As this happens, it disrupts almost every industry and creates economic opportunity for those who are able to either build new organizations or retrofit existing businesses to accommodate these changes. In this chapter, I cover five industry trends that illustrate how value is created in the Purpose Economy, and how it will continue in the future.

I. Retail
In her now-famous TED talk, musician Amanda Palmer points out that "throughout history, musicians and artists have been parts

of the community—the connectors and openers."² They played a special role in the community, because their livelihood required connecting with their audience and asking for help. This deep connection to the community created vulnerability. If people didn't like the show, they were free to offer nothing for it; not to mention, they could jeer at the artists, even becoming brutal. And yet, artists also could build relationships with their fans directly through the community. By contrast, modern celebrity artists tend to hide behind agents and labels, and they must create strategies to help their audience feel connected.

When Amanda was kicked off her label for selling only 25 thousand copies of her debut album in the first two weeks—a number the label considered much too small—she found another way to move forward. When a fan came up to her at a concert, confessed to having illegally downloaded her album, and gave her a $10 bill, the small gesture sparked a big idea. For years, she had been connecting with her audience and exchanging her music for their support in the form of sofas to sleep on and home-cooked meals. As so many of Amanda's fans offered up their homes and food freely, she realized that people felt her music was helping them, and that they wanted to help her in return. After her fan volunteered to pay her for the free album he'd burned, she decided to make her music free and to open up to her community, asking them to support her directly. She launched a Kickstarter campaign to support the making of her next album, and it generated nearly $1.2 million in contributions from 25 thousand people—the same number that her record label had considered so shabby.

Amanda's story perfectly expresses how people are looking for more personal domain in their lives, which she has achieved. It also demonstrates that people are looking to contribute their time, energy, and money to things that matter to them, and they find meaning in doing so.

This shift in the way we consume is not only changing the music and media industries; it is changing the way we buy everything, from groceries to holiday gifts. The era of Walmart and later Amazon has created tremendous profits for a few, but has eroded local communities, small businesses, and artisans. New companies, from eBay to Etsy to Zaarly, have enabled small businesses to thrive, rather than just putting them out of business. Even Amazon is now getting in that game by enabling authors to remove the intermediary publisher and go directly to their audience.

Human-centered technology has enabled us to reconnect with our heritage and culture, making the production of our own products possible on an entirely new scale. One of the most potentially transformative technologies is 3-D printing, which makes it possible to produce low-volume, highly customized goods on demand, making customization at scale possible for the first time. It's already enabled exponentially more people to become designers and sellers of products that meet their vision of a community's needs.

3-D Printing

In 1907, there were 9,260 books published. In 2010, just over one hundred years later, there were 316,480 books published annually, in addition to nearly 3 million ebooks.[3] At the core of this change has been the rise of personal computing and printing. Prior to 1980, you had to write a book by hand or on a typewriter. There was no way to save the written word digitally.

While 3-D printers are still early in their development (much like a 1980s dot matrix printer), the technology has the potential to create a similar revolution in manufacturing. Most homes and offices today own the equivalent of a printing press (i.e., a computer and printer). In the not-too-distant-future, homes and offices will likely have a factory—the means to design and manufacture custom products without opening an assembly line. Creating a new toy or tool will likely be about as difficult as baking a cake.

While handcrafted products, from toys to clothes to greeting cards, often cost more than their mass-manufactured counterparts, you know that in buying them, you are supporting local craftspeople. The creation of these products begets purpose for both the buyer and seller.

The new twist is that artisans can now sell their goods not only in their own communities, but globally as well. Popular online stores like Etsy, which has grown to over 20 million members and a billion dollars in sales in 2013, do not just provide purpose to creators. They also allow buyers to interact with the creators and even commission something themselves, creating more meaningful exchanges and not simply a monetary transaction.

People are also seeking more connection to their food, as evidenced by the astonishing rise in farmers' markets across the United States. Every Sunday outside the playground in my neighborhood of Park Slope, Brooklyn, the aisles of the farmers' market are packed with those looking for the best pickles in New York City, local goat cheese, or a bounty of beautiful produce grown by small-scale farmers within a hundred miles. And while the aisles may be harder to navigate than the typical chain grocery store, the popularity of these markets is undeniable. From bodega-lined urban neighborhoods to big-box store suburbs, we are seeing a longing for a meaningful connection to our food—a way to create community, connect with the growers, and heal the planet.

In the Purpose Economy, we see the circumvention of traditional retail channels, which mark up goods at several points along the food chain. An increasingly robust direct producer-to-consumer retail capacity is emerging in which any individual can sell her wares at whatever price she determines. She can use platforms like the online farmers' market Good Eggs, and process payments for the customer using products like Jack Dorsey's Square, the inexpensive mobile payment device that turns any smartphone into a credit card processor.

This new kind of commerce creates an appealing, person-to-person marketplace that empowers people to support independent artisans and allows them to find their own suppliers, which in turn lets them express themselves through the pursuit of products and producers that interest them. Technological innovations facilitate the shopping experience, transforming it from a transactional to a social and communal experience. Shopping can therefore be a form of self-expression, as well as a vehicle for social transformation and personal economic development.

Jill Epner & BALLE

Jill Epner worked for ten years in Hilton's corporate offices. She was very successful by most measures, but she was unhappy and itching to do what she loved—make food. She finally pulled the trigger, left her job, and started a baby food company. She made every mistake a first time entrepreneur makes, and though she eventually decided to shut it down, Jill says without hesitation that it was the best decision of her life.

In the process of starting and closing her business, she came to understand how difficult it was for local entrepreneurs to raise the capital needed to scale in any meaningful way. Her focus shifted to how to help others access capital and become involved in the Slow Money movement, and to find ways to increase funding options for local businesses that didn't have the same growth trajectory as Google.

Jill soon discovered the Business Alliance for Local Living Economies (BALLE) and joined their effort to work across the

U.S. to strengthen and support local economies. Her job as the Director of Community Engagement meant that she would work directly with their members—businesses and nonprofits just like the one she had founded years before. While Jill had felt isolated in her business, BALLE helps these values-driven entrepreneurs become part of a national community. They look for connectors and conveners in local economies and train them to then support hundreds of their peers in their community. These are entrepreneurs that have been operating in isolation and usually lack financial support. BALLE helps them become strong as a collective in both enabling collaboration and finding co-funding opportunities. Jill and BALLE are part of a larger movement reconnecting people to each other, their region, and their craft, and helping us to re-imagine what it means to be a consumer.

2. Real Estate

In a relatively short period of time, the smartphone has become one of the most pervasive technologies used by middle class Americans, and for Millennials in particular, it is one of the most valued possessions, allowing connection to each other and to the world. But the smartphone is increasingly evolving into more than just a device for connecting. It is enabling new forms of commerce and exchange, as well as the sharing of resources. Armed with a smartphone, any New Yorker today can find a bike or car minutes away that they can use for a small fee, a fraction of what they would pay for full ownership.

Sharing has become a way to discover more meaning (and purpose) in our lives. Money that might have been spent on owning a big house or expensive car is freed up and can be spent on experiences. It also connects us to each other in new ways, building trust and reciprocity and deepening relationships.

The popularity of sharing is also in large part about saving money. We are on the tail end of the worst economy since the Great Depression and are now accepting high, single-digit unemployment figures and depressed wages as the new normal. Millennials, who often carry mountains of school debt, have little interest in dumping all their cash into a car or in deriving satisfaction from the size of their front lawn. Simply put, they don't care as much as Boomers did about acquiring possessions. They need to find ways to make money go further.

Fortunately, the market for sharing has accelerated exponentially in the last decade, receiving a huge boost into the mainstream by Zipcar, the market leader in car sharing. More than just a niche, Zipcar was bought by rental car giant Avis. The business of sharing has become investment-worthy and is even sparking new venture capital funds, like New York-based Collaborative Fund.

And new services such as Airbnb, an online service that allows property owners to post rental listings for as short as one night, are creating whole new markets where once there were none. In 2013, 'hosts' on its platform booked five million nights in cities and suburbs across the world and in myriad types of real estate, ranging from tree houses to penthouses. The success of Airbnb has made not only the economic case for sharing resources, but the case for finding new models of ownership that reduce our consumption and increase the meaningful experiences in our lives.

Starbucks has understood this need for decades. They aimed to be the third place in our lives—the place between work and home. You share a space with others from the community, and rather than paying rent, you pay for your sharing rights by purchasing a coffee and perhaps a pastry. In return, you get a place to sit and relax, with access to free wi-fi and a bathroom—you get a community office space. Starbucks was in many ways the start of this broader sharing movement, allowing us to become comfortable with sharing office space with strangers.

Inspired in part by Starbucks and the mobility of office technology, more formal co-working spaces are popping up everywhere. There are now 800 such commercial co-working facilities in the United States, versus only 40 in 2008 and 300 only two years ago. The shared office space phenomenon is driven not only by a growing legion of independent workers searching for inexpensive or free office space, but by the deeper forces that are behind the pursuit of purpose.

Of course, many people have gone freelance, especially in the years following the financial crisis. But the growth of the independent workforce started well before the recession, and it's largely driven by people's desire to pursue more satisfying work, to gain more control over the terms of their lives and the way in which they do their work. Increasingly, they are not working in isolation, but are participating in collaborative workspaces and collaborative projects.

The Impact Hub, for example, has created spaces all over the world to encourage collaboration and support for professionals who seek to create organizations that improve the human condition. These spaces are open and designed to build community and inspire innovation, and they have been growing explosively. *The New York Times* recently pointed out that although the dream of working independently in our own homes has been gaining in popularity, ever since Alvin Toffler introduced the notion of the "electronic cottage" in his book *The Third Wave*, many of these home workers have found the isolation alienating and are looking for more connection and interaction.

NeueHouse, a new "co-working" space in Manhattan, is a mash-up of a private club and an open office space. Its members are a purpose-driven blend of a wide range of creative professions, carefully curated with the intention of stimulating collaborations, and the space includes broadcast and recording studios and a screening room. Another shared space, called Grind, describes itself as a "work space for free-range humans."

But the sharing movement isn't just confined to new models. 68 percent of Americans now have library cards—the highest rate in history. Far from being threatened with extinction due to the rise of ebooks, as some predicted, libraries have been repurposed into much more lively community spaces for work collaboration, public gatherings, and cultural events. Whether it's in our homes, our offices, or community centers, as Americans, we are finding new ways of sharing our spaces and creating more purpose and meaning for ourselves and each other.

3. Finance

Finance looks almost nothing like it did a hundred years ago. J.P. Morgan built his financial empire by lending money to people based on their character and community standing. Money was lent to neighbors based on relationships, not collateral and loan-to-asset ratios. Debt wasn't a commodity, or something on which to create derivatives. Banking was a community business. This is the way finance worked for hundreds of years until the mid-20th century.

But in 1913, when interest on personal debt became tax-deductible, it brought with it an increase in demand for loans. A few decades later, at the height of the Great Depression, the banking system crashed and led to the founding of the Federal Deposit Insurance Corporation (FDIC), which made banking attractive again and insured deposits for the first time.

Things changed even more dramatically after World War II ended. The GI Bill, the development of the suburbs, and the promise of home ownership all increased banking activity and the subsequent need for consumer credit. The late 1950s brought the development of credit scores, and it became possible to remove the risk of lending to strangers without concern about their standing in the community or their character.

Fast forward to the 1990s, which brought the massive failure of savings and loan associations, with 747 out of 3,234 in the country going belly-up in a few short years. And less than two decades later, Wall Street fell on its face for being over-leveraged, and also for having consolidated banking to the extent that the big banks were deemed "too big to fail."

While technology and the ability to manage huge sets of data led to much of this hubris, it is also providing the likely solution. Entrepreneurs like Jeff Stewart saw an opportunity to return to the roots of finance and live up to the ideals of pioneers like J.P. Morgan. Online social networks, he figured, could enable people again to borrow money based on their character and standing in the community. In founding Lenddo, he not only saw the opportunity to create a more sustainable and sane form of banking, but also to serve the 2 billion people around the world who are currently "under-banked."

The future of personal and small business finance is social. By making banking social again and using technology to make it efficient, we can not only boost demand, but also increase the efficiency and reliability of underwriting and collections. By involving the community in deciding who gets a loan, it creates a selection bias, as people are more self-aware about the debt they should be taking on when it is transparent to their community. And when people's repayments impact the ability of their friends and family to borrow, they are much more likely to make their payments.

Lenddo now focuses on lending to the middle class in developing countries, a population that is under-banked but also lives in regions with flexible government regulations that enable the innovation. And while most of their loans are modest by American banking standards, a $500 loan can make the difference between an education or having the ability to start a business. Lenddo now has 400,000 members across 38 countries and boasts loan rates that are the same or lower than traditional lenders.

Social lending significantly removes the bank from the equation. Reputation connects borrowers and lenders directly, which eliminates the power of the intermediary and represents an opportunity to grow the lending market tenfold. Social lending reaches new populations, but in a way that is far less prone to Wall Street-style meltdowns. If social lending continues to grow at current rates, consumer and small business lending will in the near future look more like Facebook than Citibank, and will be transacted on phones. And as banking laws change, we are likely to see finance become the core revenue generation strategy of social media companies.

4. Education

We are seeing a similar shift happening in education. Homeschooling is growing seven times faster than enrollment in traditional K–12 schools. And while homeschooling isn't necessarily the solution, it is a harbinger of what is happening in the field and where America is headed.

> The modern education system is based on a manufacturing model. In 1899, the United States Commissioner of Education celebrated the fact that education had been transformed into the "appearance of a machine." He marveled that each student was now taught to "behave in an orderly manner, to stay in his own place, and not to get in the way of others."

In 1900, only six percent of teenagers graduated from high school, and it wasn't until 1918 that elementary school was compulsory across the country. With the influx of new students, schools began to grow, and so did the need for classrooms and common processes to manage them. Cars further accelerated this process by enabling the consolidation of school districts. In 1940, there were over 117,000 school districts in the country. Fifty years later, that number had shrunk to 15,000—less than 10 percent of what existed in 1940. People could travel further and faster to work and school, which made it possible to have one district cover more territory.

By the end of the century, the number of teenagers graduating from college had boomed to 85 percent, achieving the goal of inclusion.[4] But it came at the cost of turning our schools into factories optimized for scale and efficiency. My children's Brooklyn elementary school has ten kindergarten classes, ten first grades, ten second grades, and so on. The teachers are heroic, but the system and scale is constantly a battle to overcome. This reality was made even more acute in the Information Economy, when it became viable to start using big data to evaluate schools. With the No Child Left Behind Act and then Race to the Top, the pressures from the system on teachers to conform and commoditize education have compounded.

Kids are getting lost in the factory. The massive school system has done such a great job in scaling and efficiency that it has lost the ability to serve an individual child. That is, in an effort to scale our education system, we've sacrificed quality in the pursuit of quantity. Schools, like banks, have come to rely on data rather than relationships. The parents who decide to yank their children from schools and teach them at home are simply fed up. They want to create a rigorous and personalized educational experience for their children, and given the cost of private schools, taking matters into their own hands is the only viable option.

Fortunately, new platforms and technology have made homeschooling manageable on many fronts. Parents can do everything from accessing first-rate courses online to finding support from other parents in the same situation. The best part is that they can completely tailor the experience to the learning style and interest of their children and give them the attention that they would never get in the classroom. The results are striking. 25 percent of homeschooled children are at least one grade ahead of their traditionally schooled peers. The homeschooled population as a whole scores exceptionally higher on academic achievement tests.[5] This shift is perhaps the best glimpse of the future of education—mass customization alongside personalized attention. Like banking, it will return to a human-scale model based on relationships and personal needs, and it will be where much of the disruption in the economy and labor market occurs in the next few decades.

I was very fortunate to attend Community High School in Ann Arbor, Michigan. Unlike the other two high schools in Ann Arbor, each with thousands of students and located in residential neighborhoods, Community High School is small (with 300 students at the time of my attendance) and integrated into downtown. The school embraced experiential learning and apprenticeship. For example, for every hour a student worked at a learning-based job, they could receive a half hour of classroom credit. I received high school credit for the first business that I started at 16, a baseball card dealership. Students could also recruit their own teachers from the community to learn subjects unavailable in school and receive credit for them. The school had developed a process to make learning part of the community and not isolated to the classroom.

This isn't really an innovative model; until recently, people learned primarily through apprenticeships and experience. However, those practices began to fade as schools became scaled for efficiency, as schools couldn't make them efficient. But this too is changing. It is driven in part by a greater appreciation for this style of learning, but even more so by the college admissions arms race. Doing well in high school is no longer enough to get into a good college. It requires a robust and impressive set of extracurriculars, from jobs to volunteering to international travel. This reality has changed high schools in many cities and is forcing them to create more opportunities in the community for their students.

And just as extracurriculars are necessary to get into college, finding a good job out of college now also requires a lot more than a 4.0 GPA. In fact, Google recently announced that GPA doesn't even correlate to the success of their hires. On top of studying on campus, more college students are also studying abroad, interning, and volunteering. They find all this necessary to not only land a job at graduation, but to obtain the education and self-awareness they desire.

Kristy Timms, an intern who supported me in writing this book, is a great example of this change. She chose her college almost entirely based on the school's ability to enable learning outside the classroom. She attends CUNY's Macaulay Honors College because is it committed to supporting students learning outside the classroom, and it's situated in New York City, where opportunities are abundant.

Kristy loves classroom learning, but although it can lay a theoretical foundation, she has found it lacks in helping people understand how to apply their learning to the real world. By combining the classroom learning with internships, she is able to get a complete education, and Macaulay encourages and supports this approach. The other colleges Kristy researched, especially those that are campus-focused, just couldn't compete. She has now completed internships in different sectors and is able to narrow her interests and focus her academic plan. Through internships, she was exposed to topics that, while not on her radar, captivated her and influenced the courses she took the following semester.

By working in different sectors, roles, and sizes of organizations, Kristy is incredibly self-aware for someone her age. When she graduates, she will not only have an impressive resumé, but her maturity and confidence will place her at the top of the pack. Perhaps most importantly, she has come to appreciate that life is a journey, and that she can work in many places and environments in her life and find deep purpose in them.

5. Health Care

Another field undergoing a radical transformation is health care, which also spent much of the last hundred years focused on scaling and efficiency. Drug stores have been around since the Middle Ages, but it wasn't until the 1920s and the inventions of insulin and penicillin that pharmaceuticals began to be mass-manufactured. In the 1950s, the industry really took off; it then boomed in the 1970s, when the patent protections for pharmaceutical companies became broader, enabling them to see returns on the massive research and development costs associated with bringing a drug to market.

It was during these decades following World War II that the health insurance industry came onto the scene. Health care evolved from a fee-for-service model, where people covered their own costs, to a model where insurance companies began to have incredible power over the industry by controlling the purse strings. Again, scale and efficiency became the goals of the day, and medical professionals, like teachers and bankers, moved from a model based on individual outcomes to one based on metrics.

My wife and I belong to One Medical Group, a start-up out of San Francisco. It provides a level of service that I frankly have never experienced at a doctor's office before. There is no wait time. Their scheduling is fully online, the doctors give out their email addresses, and physicians don't rush you out of the door. You feel like you are the only patient they are seeing that day. They hope to shift back to a model that prioritizes the relationship between the doctor and patient. By leveraging technology, they are able to free up doctors' time to focus on patients and even interact with them over email for routine issues. The average doctor sees 25 to 30 patients per day; at One Medical, the number is closer to fifteen.

But the future of medicine is even more progressive. In the early 1960s, 40 percent of doctor-patient meetings were house calls. By 1980, it was less than 1 percent. Within 25 years, house calls are likely to be the norm again, but in a very different way. Kaiser Permanente is a health care provider to 9 million Americans. Like One Medical, they are working to use technology to strip out the paperwork that dominates medical offices today. Their vision is to go even further and implement technology to enable doctors to once again visit people in their homes. Their goal is to make it the expectation of all patients to have safe, in-home care. They are working to make telemedicine and in-home monitors the new norm. Health care will again be patient-centric.

This patient-centric goal is combined with a larger shift in the medical community toward preventive care. Preventive care is not only seen as a way to save lives, but to help avoid the costs associated with chronic disease. It is increasingly clear, for example, that it is cheaper to prevent someone from getting diabetes or heart disease than it is to treat them. Unlike modern medicine, where the tendency is to throw pharmaceuticals and procedures at every problem, preventative medicine is social in its nature. It requires understanding and working with people in the context of their lives and work. In other words, it focuses on relationships.

10
Working with Purpose—
The Purpose-Driven Professional

"Emerging leaders are looking for one thing above all else in a career: purpose."—Liz Maw, President of Net Impact

Leaving the Matrix

Technology has enabled the creation of huge, global companies, where professionals become further and further removed from both suppliers and customers and from the realities of their customers' lives. Management has also become more a matter of depersonalized data analysis, of how much we're getting done and also of what we should do, undermining the role of human evaluation and creativity.

The current economic recession is also in large part a product of this structural flaw. We created a new management class that was so far removed from reality that managers stopped making rational decisions. The housing industry stopped building houses with the intention that they become long-term homes and the source of financial stability for families, and began building in excess for speculation and profit. The banking industry stopped limiting loans to amounts that people could actually afford, and began deluding not only the public, but themselves as well, about the risks that those loans would turn sour. They made money from the elaborate manipulation of information processed through highly arcane mathematical calculations and divorced from fact, with no caution about the potential impact on the lives of actual people. They had created the Matrix, operating in a parallel universe with 100 percent head and no heart.

While the reliable income from working in a traditional company is alluring, for most people, working in the Matrix is not fulfilling. Gallup-Healthways Well-Being Index, which has been polling more than 1,000 adults every day since 2008, shows that Americans feel worse about their jobs today than ever before. Gallup also reports that 71 percent of our workforce is disengaged, and 25 percent of this group is comprised of what they call CAVE-dwellers, an acronym for Consistently Against Virtually Everything.[1]

Sadly, most managers are clueless about what motivates their team. When asked to identify what their employees want, the top three things cited are good wages, job security, and promotion opportunities. When employees are actually asked, they report the top three as appreciation, feeling 'in' on things, and an understanding attitude. Not only did managers fail to identify these as the top drivers, they put them at the bottom of the list.[2] People increasingly reject the notion that success is solely about money, as well as the idea that we have to make our money first, and then we can begin making our contributions to society.

In a now-infamous interview with the *Sunday Times*, the then-CEO of Goldman Sachs professed that he, as a banker, was doing "God's work." He is likely not alone among CEOs who share the same sentiment and can point to examples to back up their claim. But for the most part, it is not purpose that truly drives the work of their companies, and they often readily abandon the interests of Main Street. Many business leaders have convinced themselves that the best way for them to contribute is to make a great deal of money and then do payback.

Will Work for Social Change

Nathaniel Koloc, co-founder of the nonprofit recruiting company ReWork (a Purpose Economy organization), graduated from college in 2008 and like most of his peers, was determined to find work that had a positive impact on society, while still being professionally challenging and rewarding. Nathaniel founded ReWork to help his peers find the jobs he found challenging to identify as a recent graduate.

Nathaniel works to help professionals find purpose-rich work through ReWork. He finds that candidates are looking for three things:

- **Legacy.** A sense that after they have done their work, be it a project, a job, or a career, the world is different in a way that is meaningful to them.

- **Mastery.** A deepening of skills, strengths, and talents that they feel help define them and their identity. This includes the increasing responsibility that comes with expertise and experience.

- **Freedom.** They want to get paid what they are worth, but they value things like remote work, flexible hours, and great benefits more than the actual size of their paycheck.

Nathaniel saw that the economic landscape of the last decade has led to an ongoing state of uncertainty within established organizations as well as start-ups, dimming the prospects of long-term job security. As careers continue to fragment, jobs are more often viewed as stepping stones along a much longer career "journey," which also explains the shift in priorities. Professionals of all ages—not just the Millennial generation—are finding that they are willing to walk the winding path of determining where their skills and backgrounds may be most useful in making the world a better place.

When Purpose Evaporates

One of my favorite questions asked of Silicon Valley executives examines the incredibly low philanthropic engagement of tech companies. Why is there a purpose void in these companies? Their answers varied, from describing entrepreneurs as Ayn Rand-style libertarians to explaining that the Valley operates in a bubble.

One insight on the issue came from David Hahn, Vice President of Product Management at LinkedIn. He observed that on the opposite end of the spectrum, employees at single-product, first-generation companies do feel rich in purpose. They are trying to disrupt the status quo and have a strong sense that their work matters. They have a sense of impact greater than themselves, are growing quickly, and are part of a vibrant tribe. Those are the three core ingredients; there is, in fact, no real purpose void.

When I was working for early-stage Silicon Valley start-ups, I had a deep sense of purpose. The first place I worked, HomeShark.com, was working to revolutionize the mortgage industry by taking the power out of institutional banking and putting it in the hands of consumers, so they could make better decisions about financing their homes. After a couple of months writing online tutorials on home buying, I was moved into a product management position. It was a dream job. I was on a constant learning curve, and I was being mentored by one of the best in the industry. By the time I was 24, I had designed, built, and launched multiple products. I had helped acquire another company and integrated its product line, which I was then responsible for managing. I was also managing a team and working across the now 200-person companies to realize the potential of my products. It was exactly as David described.

But what happened at HomeShark is what happens to most growing companies: they turn from David into Goliath. That is, as a company starts to become a leader in the market, it becomes a struggle for employees to find purpose simply by "fighting the establishment." If you look at the Silicon Valley companies that are philanthropic and have volunteer programs, they are nearly always past the 'David' phase and are now 'Goliaths'. They are too big to be tribes and typically haven't found ways to take the key evolutionary step to become communities.

In this regard, it's easier for an entrepreneur to create a Purpose Economy, David-type organization than it is to transform a 'Goliath' into a Purpose Economy company. Furthermore, as a small organization, a 'David,' it is much easier to participate in the Purpose Economy.

When a company becomes the 'Goliath,' they usually start corporate foundations and volunteer programs. They need to supplement purpose, as they are no longer consistently delivering it to employees. Jessica Rodell at the University of Georgia found that "when jobs are less meaningful, employees are more likely to increase volunteering to gain that desired sense of meaning."[3] As the organization grows, this becomes more acute. Goliaths like Hewlett-Packard or Wells Fargo, who long ago lost their David-like mojo, grew so large that employees struggled to find opportunities to grow and challenge themselves. Job growth is one of the core drivers of purpose for people, and when this too is limited, it's an uphill battle to find purpose.

One designer from Hewlett-Packard summed it up beautifully for me when he applied to do pro bono design work with the Taproot Foundation. He had been at the company for about a decade. He had steady income, worked with good people, and always had access to the best technology and tools. But there was one thing that got him thinking about leaving: he was tired of only designing in blue and white. As a designer, he craved a bigger palette; he wanted to be able to use red, green, and purple.

This lack of opportunity for self-expression motivated many of our pro bono consultants. Some were designers, but others were different kinds of artists—marketing managers, project managers, engineers, photographers, and so on. They were passionate about their craft, but working at a single company was forcing them to always utilize the same palette. And while consistency is critical to running a large company efficiently and effectively, for talented and creative professionals, it can be deadening. So many companies yearn for more innovation and creativity, but they don't take the very first critical step—thinking of their employees as artists.

Purpose-Powered

The University of Pennsylvania's Adam Grant did a very simple but powerful experiment with university fundraising call center employees. He broke them into three random groups. The first was read stories from previous call center employees about how the job had helped them develop their sales skills. The second set was told stories about how alumni had benefited from the donations raised by the call center. The third, the control group, had unrelated stories read to them.

He replicated the study five times and found the same results. Those who were read the second story, the one about purpose, more than doubled the dollars raised. By sharing a five-minute story, he doubled their impact. He had purpose-powered them.

More importantly, he had demonstrated just what middle management in large companies needed to take small steps toward evolving into Purpose Economy companies. He had given them a low-cost and easy way to create immediate results.

Seeking Purpose Outside the Organization

Rather than just volunteering to find purpose outside their day job, many professionals are leaving the role of employee all together and living in a constant state of start-up. As of 2009, more than 17 percent of the fourteen million self-employed workers in the United States considered themselves independent contractors or freelancers, concentrated heavily in sales, IT, creative services, marketing, and operations.[4] The drive to be more purposeful explains much of the momentum behind the massive exodus from mainstream corporate life. As Generation X and Millennials have entered the workforce, more professionals have created alternative ways to do work that is meaningful.

Fabio Rosati, the CEO of Elance, which connects freelancers with work, has seen the rise of this movement firsthand. There are many different benefits to freelance work, but at its core, Fabio sees the drive for meaning. Fabio was raised in Florence, Italy, and likes to compare the freelance movement to the Renaissance. He understands that most freelancers are a kind of artist, specialists of their crafts. Having developed that talent, they don't require the girding of a company, or a cubicle and a desk; they prefer to work without them. As did artists in Renaissance Florence, he points out, they must sell their art, which means they must grow and maintain a portfolio of clients who subsidize their craft.

There are, of course, plenty of people who have become freelancers out of necessity, especially in the wake of the financial crisis, and Fabio points out they tend to have a different perspective about their work, seeing it still as a more conventional job. But for those who have come to freelance out of choice, he sees that they've done so largely out of the desire to gain more control over their destiny, and in turn, their source of purpose.

When asked if they would prefer a more traditional work environment, fewer than one in ten independent contractors indicated they would prefer to return to a traditional work arrangement. Elance refers to the shift to freelancing as the "work differently," and finds that so many have chosen the freelance path because they are put off by the strictures of corporate life and want to have the latitude to select their clients.

Fabio also sees that freelancers are often driven by the satisfaction of helping others deal directly with their clients. They are generally individual contributors, and they take great satisfaction from helping others, whether that's an entrepreneur trying to realize her vision or someone at a corporation who couldn't possibly keep up with the volume of work that so many are now expected to handle. They also enjoy helping one another, and increasingly they are coming together and working in loose configurations to pool their talents.

Synthesis Corporation, run by my friend Ari Wallach, has created a new model for the orchestration of consulting. He works with large organizations including CNN, the State Department, and the National Resources Defense Council on their strategies, all with a staff of one—himself. Ari has made it his business to know the best freelancers out there and work with them to manage projects that would traditionally require large firms. Ari's model is the new model for professional services. People aren't creating a new version of Bain or McKinsey; they are working on their own and learning to build a network of freelancers to support them.

More people are creating portfolio careers where they craft their own jobs. Fabio notes that as Millennials have entered professional life, a new kind of work force has emerged in which the majority won't have a traditional career or work for one company for long stretches of time. These purpose-driven professionals are largely untethered from corporations and focus more on doing work they have a passion for. In this way, they are more like their own organizations, getting hired for projects but at their core remaining independent.

This shifting work identity is changing some of the most basic assumptions of workplace management. For an organization in the Purpose Economy, the definition of talent is incredibly broad. It includes the traditional employee, it includes freelancers, and it increasingly includes volunteers or users. Building a thriving organization means being able to know when to engage each of these groups to get the job done, while building a passionate and resilient culture that isn't confined to your four walls.

Post-Human Resources

Debbie Cohen, a veteran of the Information Economy, joined the Mozilla team in 2011 as their Head of People. From the start, it was clear that Mozilla had a different culture and leadership style that would require her to design a new approach. It was an exciting opportunity to really push the limits of management and work culture. How do you develop leaders who succeed by following rather than directing? How do you build a community in which the line between volunteers and employees is razor-thin? These kinds of questions starkly contrast the approach to human resources at most Information Economy companies like Microsoft and Amazon.com, managing people through competition, top-down hierarchy, and intellectual jousting.

Human resources, a function in organizations that we take for granted, is actually a relatively new field. A related function existed in the Industrial Economy, but human resources is largely a field that emerged in its current form in the 1980s. In many ways, the very term exposes the inherent challenge in the field. How do we treat people as human while seeing their value simply as a resource?

Personnel, the predecessor to HR, was designed to enable a company's negotiation with labor unions; it was the voice of management in containing costs and grievances. As the Information Economy emerged, businesses began to see the need to maximize their human resources, but with roots in labor negotiation and risk mitigation, HR as a whole continued to treat employees as commodities. This lack of vision was exacerbated by shifts in employment law that pigeonholed HR as an arbiter of compliance, deriving much of its organizational power from fear of litigation.

It's not a stretch to say that HR has few fans in contemporary organizations. The field has been eviscerated in the media, often depicted as management's henchmen and an impediment to innovation. This creates a real opportunity, described in the final chapter of this section, for more strategic HR professionals to redefine their role in organizations as something akin to a community manager. It changes not only how we think about talent, but also how we approach the core administrative functions that traditionally supported an organization's most important relationships—those with its people.

"Emerging leaders are looking for one thing above all else in a career: purpose," Liz Maw, President of Net Impact, shared with me. Net Impact is perhaps best described as the trade association for purpose-driven business professionals, with chapters all around the world and thousands of members. Liz explains that "to attract top talent, it is an imperative for employers to understand that the game has changed and the economy with it."

II
Leading with Purpose

The most important factor in Mozilla's success has been its audacious goal: to create Internet for the people, by the people. It was a statement of a vision for the world, but also a clear battle cry from Mozilla against the Goliath that stood in its way. Super-sizing the ambitions for a project or organization is a powerful draw; it pulls in talent to join your efforts and propels them forward with you as a team. Dreams for how your work will change lives and communities also act as powerful magnets for financial investment. It is much easier to resource an audacious idea than a modest one.

This does not change with financially-driven businesses. Modest business ideas might get a bank loan, but an audacious idea will require more risk, often in the form of venture funding. The top talent and largest financial investments are made in the biggest ideas—even if they are risky. The same is true with all Purpose Economy organizations.

When I left Chicago and moved to Silicon Valley, I had a simple question in mind. How do we ensure all nonprofits have what it takes to scale and achieve their missions? But it was my experience, first at dot-coms and then in conversations with nonprofit leaders, that transformed my initial question into a riskier but ultimately more game-changing venture.

Elaine Mason, then a vice president at MTV, now at American Express as vice president of their organizational development department, greatly affected my thinking at that time. I met Elaine shortly after we had opened our office in New York City. She had started her career in the nonprofit sector and—like me and so many others—left in frustration. It wasn't due to lower compensation; it was a result of the lost opportunity and growth potential. Elaine saw the potential for Taproot to not only make nonprofits more effective by providing pro bono work, but to actually help transform the whole nonprofit sector by attracting and retaining the best talent. How much more appealing might work in the sector be if nonprofit organizations had reliable access to the same marketing, technology, and management resources as leading companies?

That was the goal of the Taproot Foundation when we launched in 2001. We weren't looking to provide volunteers to nonprofits. We weren't just looking to help nonprofits in the Bay Area. We weren't looking to change the way companies leveraged their talent for good. We were set on ensuring all nonprofits across the nation had the resources they needed to thrive. Ultimately, our vision became that by 2020, high-quality pro bono service would be available everywhere, and all the key business professions would have adopted the pro bono ethic. It was an audacious goal to set for ourselves—bold, but not quixotic—and it has been the north star that has guided us through so many difficult challenges.

If we don't set super-sized goals at the outset, we're almost certain not to achieve them.

In committing to Taproot's vision of all businesses adopting the pro bono ethic, I drew from a well-established precedent set by others who had pursued an ambitious goals to achieve the unachievable.

When Wendy Kopp founded Teach for America, she started the game-changing organization by "suspending the laws of the universe."[1] She didn't start small, either. As a senior at Princeton, she decided she needed to create a national teaching corps and set out to raise $2.5 million. She had a huge idea, and it needed huge resources. It was this bold audacity that earned her meetings with executives from Xerox, IBM, AT&T, MetLife, and the Dodge Foundation. Wendy faced plenty of challenges along the way, but the size of her vision propelled her past them and rallied people and resources to build the organization she knew was needed to achieve her vision.

This kind of thinking propels many successful ventures in the Purpose Economy. While people will always find satisfaction from small wins (and they're important steps in any truly novel or influential achievement), it's the big, hairy, audacious goals that ignite commitment and overcome the pessimism from intermediary failures. We are all busy, and our resources are stretched. It's the historic opportunities that spur us to change our priorities and let our purpose prevail.

Pursuing a more moderate goal can actually cripple you. One thing the dot-com era taught me was the importance of framing your work in terms of potential—you didn't get investment unless you could prove you could change an industry or create a new one. If you just wanted to create a nice business, you went to the bank for a loan. If you want to aim for the stars, you need rocket fuel.

Removing Silos

For Bo Fishback, the CEO of Zaarly, it's hard to differentiate between employees and customers. Zaarly is an online marketplace that connects consumers to local food, homemade goods, wellness programs, and other services provided by their neighbors. The hundreds of business owners with Zaarly storefronts are, like Bo's employees, counting on him for their livelihood and the realization of their dreams. Both are vital to the success of his company. At any given time, Bo reports that several customers will be in their office, either co-designing the latest additions to the Zaarly platform or working on their own storefronts.

The emerging model, where an organization's community cuts across employee, contractor, and customer lines, is increasingly common in the Purpose Economy. It is designed to build long-term communities that support the mission of the firm. But what's really radical about it is that at any given time, a member could simultaneously be a shareholder, customer, and employee. The blurring of customer and employee isn't only happening with 21st-century-born companies. Even for companies like Ford, customers are increasingly driving sales, generating input for new services, and building the company's brand. People want to know what their friends and contacts think, do, eat, read, listen to, and buy, because often, "this will be similar to how they want to think, act and buy."[2] Customers make up a crucial part of the value generation process.

Other traditional organizational lines are disappearing as well. Marketing and HR have traditionally been the two core functions in a company concerned with people. They both focus on how to attract and engage people in the mission of the company, and for a long time they have been able to operate in a largely disconnected fashion, but that is becoming less possible or desirable. Smart companies today have started to think of these roles in less siloed ways, instead combining the functions to be in service of the larger community as a whole. By combining these functions, organizations are not only more efficient and effective, they become something far more important, more human-centered.

A Tale of Two Gongs

Zaarly and Yelp are both in roughly the same business: connecting consumers to the services and products in their vicinity. They also share a key cultural practice: they both bang gongs to celebrate wins. What is telling, however, is the occasion for striking the gong. At Yelp, it is hit to celebrate when the company closes an advertising deal. At Zaarly, it is hit when the company learns that one of its sellers has been able to quit their day job because of the business generated by their Zaarly storefront. Zaarly is a purpose-driven organization that celebrates the success of its community, which in turn builds deep loyalty and a community of employees and customers who are equally committed to Zaarly's success.

Community Organizing

Community organizing is the art of motivating and leading people to lead themselves. It is leadership in its purest form. Or, as Harvard's Marshall Ganz more eloquently defines it, community organizing is "the act of accepting responsibility for enabling others to achieve purpose in the face of uncertainty." There is perhaps no greater expert on community organizing than Marshall Ganz. He is largely credited with designing the wildly successful grassroots organizing strategy for Barack Obama's 2008 run for president. By then, he had been organizing for over 40 years, beginning with civil rights work in Mississippi and then under the mentorship of one of the greatest organizers in history, Cesar Chavez.

This kind of community leadership is essential to the success of an organization like Mozilla, where there is little distinction between employees, freelancers, volunteers, and users. Everyone is part of the community. For example, volunteers do much of the technical support for their products, such rolling out their mobile platform in Latin America with no staff on the ground, and training staff at cell phone stores on the new mobile browser. Volunteers, many of whom work 40 hours a week at companies like IBM, spend their nights and weekends searching for bugs in Mozilla's software.

The complexity of the Mozilla community manifested in full effect in the fall of 2013, when they hosted an 1,800 person team summit. Unlike most retreats, this one took place at three locations around the world simultaneously, and the majority of attendees were volunteers, not employees. Mozilla paid to fly and house their top volunteers to participate in a multi-day summit, soliciting their input on nearly every aspect of the organization, including their strategy. At many points during the 2013 summit, there were major disagreements; volunteers and employees passionately argued about the direction of the organization. But rather than step in and resolve the issues or force decisions, the Mozilla leadership created space for the disagreements to play out—they trusted the community to resolve the issues. Rather than prescribe top-down solutions, they allowed the solutions to come from the bottom up.

LivePerson: Building a Community of Connectors

LivePerson enables companies to connect proactively in real-time with their customers via chat, voice, and content. Founded in 1997, it was built around the insights that the new online markets still required a connection between customers and a real live person to complete their purchase or address a customer service issue. LivePerson went public in 2000, but ten years later realized it needed to make changes to its business model and expand beyond a single product line. This is a classic moment in the evolution of a successful organization. It is also a change that can dilute the culture of purpose within the organization, as the team is no longer rallied behind a single product. It often results in internal turf wars and internal politics as everyone fights for budget allocations and tries to prove their product is the crown jewel.

In 2010, LivePerson gathered the full team and jointly discussed the questions that would define their success or failure in the next evolution of the company. They knew the risk of losing their sense of purpose as they grew and diversified their product line. The lively discussion created a sense of shared reason for being—"to create meaningful connections." It also became the basis for their clarified values that revolved around community of co-owners committed to helping each other.

LivePerson hired visionary HR leader Steve Schloss to lead the transformation and elected Peter Block, the community organizing guru, to their board. Steve's tenure began with the creation of what he called the "Global Welcome Experience" for employees. Rather than a generic employee onboarding experience in a windowless conference room, he immediately put new employees in teams of five and sent them out into the community. They were each given a $50 gift card to go visit a LivePerson client and make a purchase in their store, and afterwards were asked to reflect on the experience and the interaction with the client staff. They then received another $50 gift card and performed the same transaction online. Did the online and offline experiences align? How could they be made stronger? By the end of the day, new employees understood why LivePerson exists and the value it creates.

New and existing team members created a new business card to make their mission personal. On the back of the card, employees personalized their card by completing the sentence, "I connect through _____." They found incredible diversity in how employees connected with others, from sports to imagination to making music. The mission had become personal.

As companies grow, the pursuit of purpose typically shifts from a focus on organizational purpose to purpose generated through the craft of each employee's work. LivePerson realized this was inevitable but wanted to make sure everyone maintained a common identity. UPS, an organization known for doing this well, has all their employees experience driving in a UPS truck and delivering packages. At LivePerson, Steve decided the parallel would be that regardless of their role, all employees should talk about the company and interact with customers. This would be the common shared experience, and he had them begin during their Global Welcome Experience.

The culture of a community and shared ownership began with the Global Welcome Experience but was designed to the last day an employee served on the team. If you resigned, it was your responsibility to throw your own going-away party to celebrate the community, and to express the value it played in your personal and professional development.

Building Community Leaders

Whether by choice or by force, Mozilla's leadership had to find a different model to train their leaders. Because of their unique structure, they've had to determine a way to create a bottom-up culture that could achieve success by empowering people. They had to practice servant leadership. As Head of People at Mozilla, Debbie Cohen developed a leadership program that engaged volunteers and employees side-by-side. The volunteers, many of them employees of big companies, took time off work to participate because it was such a remarkable experience and something they could not get in their day jobs.

Debbie took the program very seriously and expected the same of anyone participating. If you missed a session, you were out. The aim was to have everyone in the organization become a coach, someone who helps cultivate others so they and their teams can thrive in turn. She knew if she could reach enough managers and executives with the program in the first two years, she could create a tipping point where coaching and mentoring became the norm in their culture. Servant leadership would become the status quo.

In one of the last sessions of the leadership program, Debbie would drive the participants down to Half Moon Bay, a small town about 30 minutes south of San Francisco. She dropped them off on a street corner and told them to find a way to help someone, and that she would return at the end of the day to pick them up. She didn't set up a Habitat for Humanity build, or even identify the person or organization to help. She put the responsibility 100 percent on the participants in the moment.

They had to start talking to people and ask them if they need help. It was awkward at first. What if no one wanted their help? What would that say about them? What could they really do to help someone? They came to understand that it is an honor and privilege to serve. They realized leadership has to be earned, and doesn't just come with a title or role.

Was it the best way to provide support to the community in Half Moon Bay? Probably not. But for the participants, it was incredibly powerful, as it forced them to be vulnerable, resourceful, and genuinely engaged with people. The people Debbie picked up at the end of the day were different from those she had dropped off. They had gotten a taste of true leadership—courage, empathy, and service.

Work Without Managers

Debbie is now thinking bigger. Can Mozilla can be a community without managers? How can she create a culture of coaching and support that doesn't require a top-down hierarchy? How can she build the kind of company that truly serves its community— employees, customers, and investors?

A disintermediated workforce is not as radical as it sounds, and is an idea that several companies are experimenting with, most notably Evan Williams' new company, Medium. Evan wanted to boost creativity from his whole team, solve problems more quickly, spend less time in meetings, speed production, and have the entire team truly understand the business. As Evan describes it, as a team they define the game they are playing and how they keep scope. They then break their work into projects and nail down the goals and scope. From concept to launch, each project cuts across all parts of the organization and is tracked visually on a board in the office. No one works directly for anyone else. It is up to you if you want to take the lead to make something happen. To get help, you have to convince others to help you. Finally, they avoid all deadlines and structured meetings.

He reports it has worked remarkably well. "The team is ruthlessly focused on the right things with a fraction of the input." Admittedly, they are a small company of what Evan describes as "incredibly well-rounded individuals". But in spite of its small-scale experiment, it is inspiring others like Debbie at Mozilla, and more recently Tony Hsieh at Zappos, to push the limits of what work can and should be.

Debbie and the Mozilla team are at the forefront of the Purpose Economy and wrestling with some of the new challenges that come with it. For example, the non-engineering team members tend to be less purpose-driven. If you are working in accounting, how do you still feel like a strong part of the community? How do you design the culture where accountants can share the passion? Or, how do you fire people in an organization where employees are completely dedicated to the mission? When they have to let someone go for performance, it isn't just taking away their job; it can take away their purpose and passion. If your work is simply your job or career, that is one matter, but what if it is your calling, and your entire universe is built around that community?

Lessons from the Zoo

Stuart Bunderson at Washington University in St. Louis and Jeffery Thompson at Brigham Young University have begun to study the dynamics of purpose at work and found the perfect venue to explore these issues—at the zoo.

Zookeepers are well educated (73 percent have a Bachelor of Science degree or higher) but average less than $25,000 in income, which requires the majority of them (63 percent) to rely on other sources of income, from second jobs to family support.[3] There is no real room for advancement or moving up, and outsiders generally consider it dirty and unglamorous work. Needless to say, it is not a high prestige job.

Despite all those challenges, however, turnover is incredibly low, and many keepers even volunteer for months or years before actually getting hired. When Stuart and Jeffery asked zookeepers what would cause them to quit, few could come up with anything. "There's not much that they could do to get me to quit." "I don't think there is anything that they could do to me that would make me leave." "I can't think of what would cause me to leave."

For the zookeepers, they are part of a community and have a deep sense of responsibility to the animals. The animals have given up their freedom in order to educate the public, and the zookeepers see it as their responsibility to provide the very best care for them. If they don't care for the animals, who will? If an animal is sick, they will often skip breaks or come into the zoo in the middle of the night to care for it.

There are some clear differences between a zoo and Mozilla, but they share some critical characteristics. If an employee left one zoo, for example, where would he or she go? The jobs are few and far between, and it isn't as if there are ten other zoos hiring in the same city. In the same way, Mozilla is the community for those who are passionate about a people-oriented Internet. While there are other major open-source communities, from Drupal to WordPress, the paid gigs in these communities are very limited.

Zookeepers and members of the Mozilla community hold their leadership to a different bar than Microsoft holds for its employees. Zookeepers are hard to manage by any traditional measure. They don't see their work as a job—it's a moral duty. They see themselves as stewards of the well-being of the animals, and more broadly, of wildlife conservation.

When a traditional executive at a company like Microsoft or Bank of America makes a decision that is unpopular with the team, they are considered ineffective managers. Employees will find them guilty of poor judgment. But when an administrator at a zoo decides to spend limited resources on a new carousel or popcorn stand instead of improving the living conditions of the animals, they risk being considered immoral. In an organization that prizes purpose, management is held to a higher standard.

Purpose-driven leadership comes with great responsibility, and this is where the researchers also found a major riddle in the management of zoos. In talking to zookeepers, Stuart and Jeffery heard something that surprised them. Many zookeepers confessed to loving their work, in spite of the hard and often unpleasant conditions, but said they would never let management know; in fact, they actively gave management the impression they hated their jobs. They feared that if management knew, they could be exploited; they derived power by projecting hatred of their work. Or, more accurately, they avoided giving management the power to manipulate them by not letting them know they would work for free.

It was just like what Debbie saw at Mozilla when someone was let go and then immediately signed up to volunteer. It wasn't merely a job. The management at zoos and organizations like Mozilla don't just control paychecks; they are being given the power to have control over someone's purpose. That is an incredible onus and one that could easily be abused.

By choosing work rich in purpose, we become vulnerable. Vulnerability is at the core of being human. It will require a new kind of leadership to find creative ways to make it safe to be vulnerable. This is the riddle of leading in the Purpose Economy.

An Incremental Change—Leader as Conductor

For many, the jump to completely integrating a community may be too great a risk and too heavy a lift to do all at once. Elance's Fabio Rosati uses a conductor as a metaphor for an incremental shift in how an organization can approach leadership that points it in the right direction. As he puts it, "A conductor is not someone who tells people what to do, but rather someone who orchestrates work. A conductor is also an extraordinary motivator and is really good at understanding the skills of every person, and how these skills can be brought together."

While short of fully embracing community organizing, the leader-as-conductor metaphor creates a mental model for how to lead increasingly fluid teams comprised of core in-house staff and a distributed outside work force with highly specialized skills brought in for particular jobs. Fabio is using the model himself at Elance, where one-third of the staff is full-time and two-thirds are freelancers. He is seeing that the organizations using this model are generally doing it well, largely because people are so ready to work this way.

This doesn't mean that a Purpose Economy leader is just another member of the team. As Fabio points out, "Somebody still has to step out and say, 'Here's what we need to accomplish.'" This manner of leadership requires not only orchestration, but inspiration and empathy. Crucial to this is a deep understanding of what people are feeling, and respecting and encouraging their desire for expression, something I've found particularly powerful in building Taproot.

Learning to relinquish control and to be more collaborative isn't going to be just a choice for much longer. With the current flood of people out of the traditional workforce, and as the Purpose Economy grows larger, more of us won't be working in or leading organizations at all; we'll be crafting working groups of independent talent to tackle projects on a case by case basis.

For years, I was told by mentors that as CEO, I should be leading and not doing. The fact that I still did a lot of writing, as well as program and visual design, was seen as a founder's failure to let go. And yet, some of my most rewarding hours were doing these tasks, and frankly, the results resulted in some of our highest impact.

These tasks gave me purpose, as they allowed me to express myself. This is something few leaders give themselves permission to do, and yet it is one of the most powerful things you can do for an organization. For a recent event, I drew portraits of the one hundred attendees. It took a day to do, but made me feel connected to the attendees. In studying their faces, I saw old friends in new ways and started to relate to new friends before I met them. It made the group feel like a community and increased my empathy. It also really made an impact on their experience to receive a framed portrait that was drawn by the CEO. One attendee, a senior executive from Accenture, tweeted that it was the best event giveaway ever.

Even as a conductor, you need to occasionally pick up an instrument to play. It is a fine balance to achieve, but a conductor who never plays music stops relating to the orchestra and may fall out of love with music. It is very hard to retain a sense of purpose, or a contagious kind of passion, if you forbid yourself from being expressive and creative.

SECTION FOUR

SOCIETAL PURPOSE—MOVING MARKETS

12
Market Movers

Section One laid out the foundation for the Purpose Economy, what it is, and how it is poised to change the way we live. Section Two described the science of purpose in our careers—it helped us understand the true nature and importance of purpose in our work. Section Three outlined how organizations are changing, and how they are operating and growing in the Purpose Economy. Now it is time to get to the trillion-dollar question: How do the leaders of today move markets in this new economy?

The Purpose Economy is about more than just profits; it's about creating meaningful impact in service of people and the planet. The great business challenge now is not just how to build a successful organization, but how to build more human-centered markets. We all see how much need there is in the world, and it breaks our hearts, but it also inspires our empathy and creativity—the ability to see the need as opportunity. It is this kind of opportunity, the kind that serves people and the planet, that is fueling entrepreneurship and the transformation of old world businesses within the Purpose Economy.

The challenges and opportunities we face today are unprecedented and sometimes overwhelming in scale. Issues like climate change are part of a long list of challenges that could and likely will impact that way we live. And while we can often find solutions to address the demands of a specific community or niche population, finding a systemic solution is almost always elusive. But we can no longer delay solving the most intractable problems. If not us, then who? If not now, then when?

I believe that social challenges and the desire for self-expression and community are new market opportunities in the Purpose Economy. Just as data storage and software development formed some of the Information Economy markets, things like sustainable energy and resource sharing are emerging as Purpose Economy markets. By thinking of these as markets, we can imagine powerful new ways to create value by helping people and the planet. By using the language of economics and investment, we attract the human and financial capital needed to build and grow markets in the Purpose Economy.

In this section, I lay out a framework I developed based on over a half century of social science and economics, as well as the insights of some of the most successful entrepreneurs of the era. I believe it has the potential to help us solve some of our most difficult social problems. It provides a clear path for not only creating a wildly successful organization, but affecting meaningful change on a systemic scale. It is a step-by-step guide to understanding how to make an impact as an investor, academic, employee, or simply as a voter. It does not belong to any one sector, and it transcends organizational structure.

Electric Cars and the Diffusion of Innovations Theory

Elon Musk is the man behind PayPal, SpaceX, and Tesla Motors. He has successfully built a number of companies, but more importantly, he has moved markets. Elon Musk had a different kind of vision from the start: to build a market for electric cars, beginning with luxury cars, and then expanding over time to reach a broader consumer base. This was a rather specific vision; that is, it wasn't simply about building an amazing electric car, it was also about creating an environment in which it could be successful. Not unlike Steve Jobs, Musk is constantly designing his products and services as he simultaneously readies the marketplace for them.

Musk's vision completely aligns with a principle that scientists have known for over half a century: innovations spread socially and over time. The diffusion of innovations theory, developed in 1962 by sociologist Everett Rogers, explains how, why, and at what rate new ideas and technologies spread through populations. As a young graduate student, Everett was studying one of the hottest innovations of the day—hybrid corn seed. Specifically, he was trying to understand why some farmers were using this new improved technology, and others weren't. As Thomas Edison famously wrote to the CEO of General Electric in 1926, "It takes about seven years to convert the average man to the acceptance of a solved problem." Everett Rogers wanted to understand why this was the case.

I personally became aware of the diffusion of innovations theory in Geoffrey Moore's *Crossing the Chasm*.[1] It was a bible of technology marketing when I was working in product management in Silicon Valley in the late 1990s. By providing a model for how to target the right segments of the population for each stage of sales, the theory enabled you as a marketer to set realistic expectations about pick-up rates, and it instructed you how to send the right message at each stage of market development. It also modeled the best practice of using each group as a base to market to the next group, leveraging your existing customers to help sell to future customers. The book put a special focus on the most difficult part of getting widespread market adoption for a new technology: going from early adopters to the early majority, the tipping point for technology adoption.

The first group, the innovators, are a small group of people who actively seek out risks and new challenges. Risk (and its accompanying reward) constitutes a large part of their motivation to engage. They are the first individuals to adopt an innovation. They tend to be young, financially well-off, and highly social, with the

Diffusion of Innovations Theory

Adoption Curve

INNOVATORS	EARLY ADOPTERS	EARLY MAJORITY	LATE MAJORITY	LAGGARDS
2.5%	13.5%	34%	34%	16%
Innovators are enthusiasts, and they desire to be the first to use the latest technology. They represent a tiny percentage of the market.	Early Adopters are those who enjoy new innovations and are comfortable taking social risk but are largely motivated by its potential to drive their success. They are very influential in the marketplace, acting as trendsetters.	The Early Majority is made up of pragmatists who adopt new innovations only after it is proven and they feel comfortable that it won't put them at risk. They are the largest segment of the market.	The Late Majority are conservative thinkers who are risk averse and extremely cautious when using anything new. They not only want to see demonstrable results, they need to be reassured that there is next to no risk. They also represent a large portion of the market.	Laggards only use new technology if forced, and then do so kicking and screaming. They are a small audience.

What Everett Rogers found was that with any change, there are five types of actors who are central to its spread, or diffusion. These groups essentially represent a willingness to adopt an innovation, which Everett mapped in his now-classic 'adoption curve.'

closest contact to emerging research and data. Often, they interact with other innovators. They also tend to have a financial and social cushion that can absorb the potential losses associated with trying something that doesn't work.

Elon Musk is one of these innovators, and he understood what it would take to get that group behind the wheel of an electric car. He would need to design a car that could be compelling enough to act as a status symbol for young professionals in the insular community of Silicon Valley. He knew his audience would be highly technologically literate and very social in both how they bought the car and how they talked about it. He needed a luxury car that would be the "it" car in Silicon Valley. But perhaps as importantly, he would need to find a solution for the incredibly expensive battery technology needed for the car to work. Just the battery for an electric car costs more than double the price of an entry-level car in the market. For this reason alone, Tesla would have to focus on the luxury end of the market.

Tesla's cars are designed and built for the Google or Apple executive. The Apple headquarters boast more Teslas than a Tesla showroom. Early buyers were not price-sensitive and placed a premium on service and design. Tesla identified their innovator customer segment and focused their energies on selling and servicing them in unique ways. For example, Tesla understood the busy schedules of their customers, and had their service technicians visit owners for maintenance appointments rather than forcing them to sit waiting in a garage. Five years after the introduction of its Model S car, Tesla was reporting a profit, and the Model S had become the third best-selling luxury car, behind only the Mercedes E Class and BMW 5 Series.

But it's not just the innovators that catalyze a market. What Everett Rogers came to understand was that it is the social connection between different segments of a population that diffuse an innovation. Innovators are merely a stepping stone to the most critical group—early adopters. Early adopters are typically affluent, educated, and are motivated by social prestige. They are the proverbial tire kickers of the population, ensuring the car is safe before it gets on the road, and in turn bringing along the more risk-averse parts of the population. More so than any other group, they will determine the success of an innovation.

When early adopters around the world see Apple and Google executives driving a Tesla, they want to be the first in their city and among their peer group to drive one. Whether consciously or not, they see it as a social advantage and part of defining their personal brand. Tesla has now opened showrooms around the world in affluent communities, moving beyond California and the innovators to the next segment of the adoption curve. To further entice the early adopters, Tesla is building a network of car superchargers so that owners can drive coast-to-coast without range anxiety. And to more strongly compel these slightly more risk-averse buyers, Tesla is covering the cost of the power for these stations.

However, that is as far as Tesla has gone. The next segment it needs to reach is the early majority—who can move the company from a niche car manufacturer into a global powerhouse. When compared to the early adopters, the early majority is pragmatic, less affluent, and more risk-averse. And though they look to the previous group for guidance, they often have practical considerations that make it hard to adopt a change. Tesla is not going to be able to sell their current product to the early majority with much success; it is too expensive and not very practical. The battery range is still too short, the price too high, and their charging stations are mostly limited to corridors with high concentrations of early adopters (i.e. California and the D.C. to Boston corridor).

What Musk understands is that to move into the early majority and beyond, he needs to invest in the electric car market, and not just his cars. Tesla won't succeed just by selling electric cars. They need to grow the overall electric vehicle market. They need to remove barriers for their competitors so they can join them in moving away from gas-fueled cars. To this end, Tesla now sells their patented powertrain components to competitors. They are less concerned about the competition taking up market share than building the market and creating scale that will bring the prices down enough to be viable options for the average car buyer.

By selling luxury electric cars first, Musk and his team at Tesla have actually accelerated the development of technology for the market. Tesla's success has created further hope for electric cars and spurred investment in research and development. Musk's initial customers were largely in Silicon Valley and connected to venture funding, a proximity that ultimately increased investment in batteries and renewable energy.

But while the initial scale of his operations allowed Musk to create additional demand and begin to bring down prices, this won't be enough to bring along the late majority or the laggards. These more risk-averse groups will need power stations all around them, and ultimately it will need to be easier than owning a gas fueled car. In order for the laggards—the most risk-averse group of all—to come along, there will likely need to be policy change or simply no more gas stations left to fuel their antique cars. But if Musk's 'luxury cars for the tech-elite' strategy works, it will ultimately allow Musk to sell electric-powered sedans and minivans to families in Ohio.

It sounds intuitive, maybe even obvious, but most entrepreneurs (particularly those working on social issues) don't follow this model. They only see what is right in front of them and fail to understand the importance of building a market rather than just a product or service. More importantly, they don't have the laser focus on a single segment of the adoption curve at one time, much less the correct segment. But the diffusion of innovations theory ultimately explains adoption of hybrid corn seed, why Elon Musk first entered the electric car market by focusing on luxury cars, and other social changes like sustainability, same-sex marriage, and—in my case—pro bono services. Based on this theory, market movers build markets intuitively and with great discipline.

Same-Sex Marriage

Over two decades ago, gay marriage already had the support of innovators and early adopters. Innovators likely have always supported it either as gays themselves, libertarians, or passionate civil rights advocates. The early adopters have been coming over to the issue since the 1990s.

The battle of the last ten years, as well as the next ten, is all about the early majority, which tips the voting public in favor of the practice. They are pragmatists who are simply more cautious. They aren't necessarily against gay marriage, but might not have many openly gay friends to humanize the issue. They may not see the system as necessarily broken, as it doesn't impact them directly. Too many leaders in the civil rights movement tried to engage in public debates and campaigns to address the late majority and laggards. They got in fiery interactions about rights and morality, when that wasn't the issue for the early majority. This was likely not only a waste of time, but may have turned off some of the early majority.

What was needed wasn't a righteous and expensive battle with people who weren't even necessary to succeed. It was simply a matter of reaching the pragmatic center. This is what market movers realize. They don't engage and waste energy on the impossible just to win battles; they see the sequence of moves needed and don't try to fight battles they can't (and don't need to) win. They operate in a marketplace and understand how it works. As leaders look to move markets to advance the Purpose Economy, the diffusion of innovations theory can take a seemly chaotic, out-of-control, and random process, and make it fairly linear and predictable.

Many organizations with great ideas fail simply because they don't use the diffusion of innovations model. They think their idea is so great that they can't get out of their own head to realize not everyone is ready for it. Same-sex marriage is a perfect example of how this applies to a non-commercial innovation. It is an innovation, but not a service or product. It is a custom, but one requiring changes to public policy. To get the laws of the land to change doesn't require the later majority or laggards to be on board. The laws could be passed without their support at all. The late majority who saw it as a threat, or laggards who saw it as tantamount to the end of the earth, weren't even relevant to the conversation.

Crossing the Chasm in the Sustainable Foods Market

It wasn't long ago that the sustainable consumer products market was mostly operating on the fringes of society. In those early days, the market was really more of a movement supported by a tiny portion of the population—innovators shopping at and running small health food stores. These stores smelled like vitamins, and the organic produce sold on their shelves looked sickly. It took real dedication to shop in them.

It wasn't until the 1980s, with the introduction in the United States of visionary brands like The Body Shop, Whole Foods Market, and Ben & Jerry's, that we started to see early adopters enter the market. Unlike the early days of the sustainable products movement, these new brands found success largely by making their products more appealing to the early adopters, people who cared about health and sustainability but also wanted products that worked well and provided satisfaction.

These companies offered great products, but at a higher cost. For early adopters, this was fine. Remember, early adopters tend to be more affluent and image-conscious. They are the people we see wandering the aisles of Whole Foods Market (or as some call it, Whole Paycheck).

By 2012, Whole Foods Markets had 340 stores and 2,400 natural and organic products on their shelves. They sold over $12 billion and employed nearly 75,000 people.[2] They had come a long way from the health food stores before them.

But even with 340 stores, Whole Foods Market only serves a small part of the overall market. There are 37,053 supermarkets in the United States selling $602 billion in goods per year. That means that roughly one in a hundred supermarkets is a Whole Foods Market, and they have only 2 percent of the market share by revenue.[3]

The impact of Whole Foods Market, however, is much greater than you would infer from their size. Similar to Tesla, despite a small share of the market, they have changed the overall market and started the march toward the early majority. They have cultivated the early adopters and turned them into tastemakers that are making the early majority pay attention. As of 2013, 63 percent of Americans reported buying organic foods, and 40 percent planned to increase their purchases of organic foods in the coming year.[4] The early majority has entered the market, but their needs are different than those of longstanding Whole Foods Market customers. They need lower costs and easier access to sustainable and healthy food.

Here, Whole Foods Market again has made a tremendous impact. By selling to early adopters, they created enough demand to support hundreds of suppliers. Prior to Whole Foods Market's rise, many organic and sustainable products simply didn't have a retail channel to generate enough sales to survive. Many local family farms and niche packaged food brands simply couldn't last. Whole Foods Market created enough sales to float these businesses and to inspire many new ones. Once stable, these businesses could begin the harder push into other retail outlets.

More and more major supermarket chains now have organic products to appeal to the emerging market. By 2010, large supermarkets sold 54 percent of organic food.[5] While this is leaps and bounds from where the market was ten years ago, the selection is still limited in most stores. This remains a barrier for the early majority, who report that despite their desire to buy more organics, they often can't find them in the stores where they shop.[1]

There is a fundamental chicken and egg riddle in moving to sustainable products in supermarkets. Even if the largest retailers wanted to move to more responsible products, in most cases, they wouldn't have the suppliers necessary to stock their shelves in the volume they require. Most of the Whole Foods Market suppliers simply don't have the infrastructure to meet the needs of millions more buyers.

Out of the suppliers Whole Foods Market and their peers nurture, some of the brands take off and are able to go mainstream, to cross the chasm into the early majority market and be able to scale to meet the needs of large retailers. Seth Goldman's Honest Tea is one of the early examples of a product that made this jump.

Honest Tea was founded in 1998 to provide healthier (and later organic) iced tea products to the market. It was initially sold through Fresh Fields, later acquired by Whole Foods Market. Their first shipment to the stores was for 15,000 bottles.[6] The product quickly took off, and sales through Whole Foods were booming. It caught the attention of the king of sugary beverages, the Coca-Cola Company, who made a major investment in the company in 2008 to help it move into the larger markets. In 2009, word got out that Honest Tea was President Obama's preferred drink and was being stocked at the White House. The company was on top of the world.

By 2011, what Honest Tea found, however, was that building and managing the distribution and production necessary to fill the shelves of major retailers and reach the majority of Americans was a daunting task. It required a different kind of company. Marketing, distribution, and production would need to be its core competencies. Making great iced tea was the easy part. That same year, Honest Tea was acquired by Coke, which enabled the Honest Tea brand to sit on top of the same marketing, production, and distribution systems of Coca-Cola. Whole Foods had incubated a product that had crossed over into the majority.

This is the story of how sustainable and healthy foods move through the adoption curve. Over 50 years, suppliers went from niche health food stores catering to innovators, to the sexy shelves of Whole Foods Market, to now having their products sold by the Coca-Cola Company.

More and more companies will follow the path of Honest Tea and find ways to distribute their products by partnering with large platforms who can bring their products to the masses. Some of those platforms will also begin to create their own new products to meet this market need. But there will remain consumers and companies that will be reluctant to make the move without further incentives and infrastructure. These are the late majority and laggards.

My wife, Kara Hurst, has been at the forefront of the effort to address the needs of the late majority in this market for over a dozen years. In 2012, she was recruited to become the CEO of The Sustainability Consortium (TSC), an organization that is leading efforts to bring scientifically-based data and industry innovations to bear on the market for sustainable goods production. They are working to make sustainability viable for the early majority by decreasing risk and increasing scalability.

TSC, with a membership of over a hundred partners—around seventy-five global companies, fifteen civil society organizations, and ten or so universities—is truly global. Based in three continents, TSC is creating cohesive and efficient approaches to understanding the social and environmental impacts and improvement opportunities to product sustainability.[7] They look at all aspects of products—the full "life cycle"—from design, to materials, production and manufacturing, transportation, sale, consumer use, and disposal. They consider the social issues as well, including labor practices and human rights issues. TSC is arming major retailers like Walmart, Tesco, Marks & Spencer, and Ahold, among others, to work with their suppliers to change how we as consumers can access more sustainable products. They are creating the infrastructure to support sustainable products at a massive scale.

The market-moving power of TSC is tremendous—together they employ well over fifty-seven million people and their combined revenues total over $1.5 trillion.[7] The goal is eventually to communicate this information directly to consumers through a product label or scannable QR code, much like the nutrition labeling that is required in many markets today. In the not-so-distant future, when buying a T-shirt, laundry detergent, or even wine, consumers will be able to make informed choices in a much more standardized way than they can now. And though the sustainable goods market is now crossing over to the more risk-averse populations, there is still much more work to be done before it can reach the hardest-to-reach groups.

Cautionary Tale:
Ignoring the Diffusion of Innovations

When reading about Tesla and Whole Foods Market, building a market sounds fairly intuitive and obvious. You need to understand which segment of the adoption curve is next and then meet their needs and remove their barriers.

Sadly, my uncle, Marc Porat, was at the center of one of the greatest cautionary tales about ignoring the social science of innovation. The first iPhone was released on June 29, 2007. What very few people know is that the first real iPhone was first developed 17 years earlier, and while Steve Jobs was off working on other ventures.

In 1990, then-Apple executive Marc Porat convinced John Scully that the next generation of computing would require a partnership of computers, communications, and consumer electronics. John gave it the green light, but it was under-resourced, and by May of that year, Marc had convinced him to let it be spun out and to allow him to take two of Apple's stars (Bill Atkinson and Andy Hertzfeld) with him.

They founded a new company and called it General Magic. Within a couple of years, they launched the first smartphone. You could make calls, manage your calendar, and even shop online. To put this in perspective, this was before the first web browser and required the phone to be connected to a phone line (i.e. not so mobile).

The company went public and the stock doubled on the first day. Then it all fell apart. The market wasn't ready. The partner infrastructure wasn't in place. The company ended up seeking new business models and products, and 12 years after General Magic was founded, it ceased operations. Five years later, the iPhone was released.

> Marc had built a product for innovators, but the early adopter market wasn't going to be ready for over a dozen more years. It was too big a jump and neglected to build the market by meeting people where they were at the time. It was made all that much harder given that the technology wasn't ready to deliver a decent experience.

Putting the Adoption Curve to Work: Thinking Like Musk and Mackey

It is unlikely that Whole Foods Market's John Mackey or Tesla's Elon Musk had the diffusion of innovations curve mounted on their wall in their office to guide their work. They may have come across it at some point, but more likely, their moves were intuitive. It is the way they are wired.

Michael Brown and Alan Khazei, the founders of Boston-based City Year, developed a model and name for how to intentionally operationalize the adoption curve and put it into practice. They not only made it something anyone can do, but also a model that requires it to be a team effort and not the work of a lone entrepreneur. It made the curve accessible.

For Michael and Alan, the market they wanted to move was service. Their goal was to someday have all Americans spend a year of their life performing service for their community. While Americans are still a long way from achieving this goal, the accomplishments of the organization are remarkable. What started as a small nonprofit program in Boston led to the creation of the federal AmeriCorps program that engaged 80,000 Americans in a year of service in 2012. This includes the participants of Teach for America. Without City Year, there would be no AmeriCorps or Teach for America.

Michael and Alan describe their model as an action tank. As they explained it to me, think tanks are all talk. We need action tanks focused on specific changes in society. Tesla is an action tank. Whole Foods Market is an action tank. The concept, which they had implemented at City Year, was simple: define your audience, set a goal for them to adopt the desired change, identify the largest barriers to moving forward, and set to work to remove them.

For City Year, the audience wasn't the people doing the service. They weren't the barrier to adoptions of the market. The challenge the organization faced was money. For someone to do a year of service requires paying them a stipend to cover their basic expenses, just like the Peace Corps provides. Participants would need roughly $12,000 per year to cover housing and food and would also require training and management, which created another expense. The vision was that the program had to have a model similar to the Peace Corps. It needed to be largely government-funded.

The audience for City Year was politicians. They were the ones who needed to fund the vision. Michael and Alan knew they might convince a few innovators among the political elite to support the program, but to get to the early adopters and early majority they needed, they had to get beyond abstractly selling the idea to politicians. They needed them to experience it firsthand and see the power.

So, despite their grand vision, City Year started like most nonprofits. It launched in Boston from the ground as a small program. But unlike most nonprofits, Michael and Alan were running an action tank. They managed their program to ensure great outcomes for everyone involved, but their bigger goal was to get politicians and lobbyists (i.e. corporate leaders) to come and witness the program. They also dressed all their participants in bright red jackets they wore around town so that those same leaders would see them and get a sense of the potential.

It was on one of these tours that a presidential candidate, Bill Clinton, saw the power of their vision. Adopting their vision became part of his ticket, and when he was elected, City Year passed with relative ease, given all the support they had been building by demonstrating the potential on the ground.

Examples of Markets

ARTS
- Shared art space
- Theater

ADVOCACY
- Design
- Public interest design

ECONOMIC DEVELOPMENT

EDUCATION
- Adult literacy
- Online learning
- Self-help
- STEM education
- Bilingual education
- Adult education
- Arts education
- Educational toys
- Special needs education
- Study abroad
- Pre-K

ENERGY & ENVIRONMENT
- Alternative fuels
- Residential power usage
- Residential composting
- Water consumption
- Recycling
- Alternative packing materials
- Reforestation
- Second life for products

BUSINESS & FINANCE
- Debt reduction
- Impact investing
- Glass ceiling for women in business
- Socially responsible investing
- Cause marketing
- Entrepreneurship
- Business transparency

GOVERNMENT
- Immigrant leadership
- Political transparency
- Voting rights
- Safety net
- Balanced budgets

HEALTH
- Assisted living
- Physical activity for kids
- Bio-monitoring
- Nursing
- Cancer research
- Health education
- Home health care
- Access to care

FOOD
- Summer meals for kids
- Local sourcing/farm-to-table
- Organic food
- Vegetarian diet
- Culinary education

LAW
- Human rights
- Women's rights
- Prison reform
- Civil rights

MEDIA
- Self-publishing

PUBLIC PLACES
- Green space
- Public art
- Community meeting spaces
- Community safety

RETAIL
- Supply chain management
- Fare wages
- Support for small business

REAL ESTATE
- LEED certification

TRANSPORTATION
- Public transportation
- Bike safety
- Car sharing

TECHNOLOGY
- Genetic engineering
- Online dating
- Telecommuting
- Video conferencing
- Online networking
- Online privacy
- Proximity-based social networks
- Crowdsourcing

WORKPLACE
- Employee well-being
- Outplacement
- Freelancing
- Mentoring
- Executive coaching
- Co-working space

Pro Bono Action Tank

Taproot had been an action tank organically from day one. When I started Taproot in 2001, there were many innovators already in the field. They were diehard, pro bono junkies who, despite countless challenges, stuck with it. It would be generous to say that at the time, 50 percent of projects were ever completed. In other words, pro bono at that stage was the equivalent of buggy software or rotten organic vegetables in a 1960s health food store.

Our approach with Taproot was to create a Ben & Jerry's or Whole Foods Market—a proof point to demonstrate that pro bono could "taste good." Our goal was to move the market forward in the hopes of reaching that most coveted group: the early adopters. By 2005, we were able to solve reliability and quality issues, which created an opening for a group of visionary nonprofits and professionals to join the market. These early adopters saw how pro bono could give them an advantage, and since the experience was now solid, they didn't see much risk of wasting their time.

As Taproot begin to make headway, other solutions aimed at early adopters began to emerge, from Public Architecture's 1% program to community programs like the Jericho Road Project in New England. Public Architecture challenged architecture firms to donate one percent of their time to community projects and were able to convince 1300 firms to generate over $40 million in services per year.

Roughly five years after Taproot started, I met Michael Brown and learned of action tank framework. I was immediately sold. It was what I had been trying to do, but his team had taken it further, naming it and making something that was more accessible for a team to drive, and not just a lone entrepreneur.

An action tank was the deliverable model we needed to cross the chasm into the early majority. I now needed to make this process intentional and more accessible to my team and our friends. Taproot needed to create an action tank to realize its goal of ensuring all nonprofits had access to the professional services they need to thrive, and that all professionals saw pro bono service as core to their identity.

The Pro Bono Action Tank (PBAT) was formed, and Jamie Hartman and appointed to run it. She would form a council of the leaders in the field, and each year, they would identify the barriers to progress towards the goal and work as a coalition to remove them—or at least shrink them down to a size that would enable jumping over them.

We all worked together to build the PBAT Leadership Council, and when we launched our website, it featured many of the most influential names in corporate philanthropy, from companies ranging from Gap, Inc. to Deloitte to Capital One. The very first barrier PBAT identified was that companies were consistently reporting that they didn't do pro bono service because it was foreign and inaccessible for them. They acknowledged that while their legal team did do pro bono work, they really felt that pro bono was just for lawyers—it didn't make sense for the rest of the company. Working in the field and talking with representatives from every profession and nearly every company, we knew this simply wasn't true, but also knew that as long as this was the perception, the field wouldn't advance.

Jamie's first major task was to find examples of pro bono work happening at dozens of leading companies and post them on our site. Instead of trying to convert these companies to pro bono, we would promote the pro bono they were already doing and invite them into the club. For example, when we called Dell and spoke to them about pro bono service, the conversation would start with sharing a case study we had developed about pro bono work already done by their employees. Rather than being put off or discouraged, Dell was proud and felt like a member of the club. The same was true of company after company we contacted. Within a year of launching PBAT, not only did Jamie have close friends at nearly every Fortune 500 company, but they all had accepted pro bono services as a standing practice. Taproot had come 180 degrees from where we had been just twelve months before.

In business, ambitious entrepreneurs often illustrate their potential by showing a chart of their revenue growth that takes the shape of a hockey stick. This is the model of nearly every wildly successful business. Growth is slow and steady at first, but then hits an inflection point where the slope quickly rises for a sustained period of time. PBAT didn't boost our revenue on the trajectory of the hockey stick, but it did have a decisive effect on our impact curve. It was the accelerant that took the strong and steady impact of our work over our first years and allowed us to achieve takeoff.

In 2007, Taproot began to make an effort to reach into the early majority, starting with our White House lobbying effort to challenge all companies to provide pro bono services. Working with the American Institute for Graphic Arts, we aimed to establish an expectation that all designers dedicate 5 percent of their time to social impact work. We also began advising companies about how to build their pro bono programs. We held up early adopters like Capital One and Deloitte as examples and demonstrated the business benefits to pragmatists who needed to be sold on the real benefits and manageability of risks. In 2008, the pro bono market was sized by the Corporation for National and Community Service at $15 billion.

Then, in 2012, we realized that, like Honest Tea, we needed a bigger platform to support our desired scale. We needed the partner equivalent of Coca-Cola to have the infrastructure to move the field to the next stage. We found that partner in Reid Hoffman's LinkedIn, which has partnered with Taproot to use their technology and network to drive deeper into the early majority. They are now developing new ways to engage their millions of members in pro bono and board service.

An Action Tank Challenge

The action tank model can be applied to any market in the Purpose Economy. It can be used for commercial opportunities, ones that are purely philanthropic, and everything in between. Here is an opportunity for you to test your skills as an action tank leader. Give it a shot.

The Market for Adopting a Vegetarian Diet

As of 2008, 7.3 million Americans (3.2 percent) were vegetarian, and 22.8 million people (10 percent) report largely following a vegetarian-inclined diet. Another 12 million (5 percent) said they were definitely interested in becoming vegetarian in the future.[9]

Your action tank's goal is to increase the percent of the Americans who are vegetarian—people who don't eat animals. The consumption of animal products is one of the largest drivers of environmental damage, from water pollution to deforestation to greenhouse gas emissions.[10] It is also linked to many of our health epidemics, including obesity, diabetes, heart disease, and cancer.[11] You want to heal the planet and our bodies by boosting vegetarianism.

Questions to ask yourself:

- Where on the adoption curve is the adoption of a vegetarian diet?
- What is the next segment that needs to be engaged to advance adoption?
- Given the likely psychological profile of this segment, what barriers need to be removed to engage them?
- How can you remove these barriers?

In the final chapter of this book, I cover how to best answer this last question. How do you move from identifying a barrier or opportunity to finding the right strategy to make it happen? As you read, consider the vegetarian case and how it applies to the barriers you identified.

13
The Five Ways to Move a Market

I have the honor of serving on business plan and social innovation competition panels regularly, and it has been amusing to watch aspiring entrepreneurs, one after another, year after year, share how their mobile application is going to make a billion dollars and end poverty. Apparently, technology and mobile applications can answer every challenge and seize every opportunity.

Technology is awesome, but it isn't the only game in town. Technology is but one of five levers, including research and data, bright spots, public perception, and policy, all of which can affect markets in the Purpose Economy. Based on my research, which was published in 2012 in the *Stanford Social Innovation Review*, market creation requires that at least three of these levers be deployed at different times or simultaneously. They are the ways you remove barriers to adoption of the changes you want to make.

My research was inspired by seeing so many brilliant people working to create real change in the world and falling short. I wondered if there was a predictable formula for successful efforts. That is, what were the secrets of systemic change? In studying successful market moving efforts, a clear pattern emerged. With every successful market-moving effort my team and I studied, we found they drew from these same five strategies or levers. Just as with Everett Rogers' diffusion of innovations, harnessing the five levers would allow a more predictable framework to move markets.

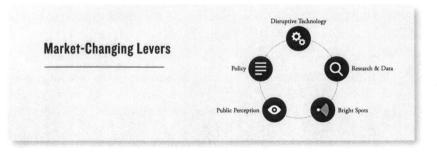

I. Bright Spots

Bright spots, or positive deviants, are examples of usually small-scale efforts that have achieved a remarkable result. They point to the possibility that something better is possible and create a starting place for thinking about replication, and how to build or expand a market. For example, in 1994, Alice Waters, a famed chef in the Bay Area, worked with a local school to create a garden for students. They called it an "edible schoolyard," and it helped to inspire the growth of the market for healthy schools. Her bright spot appealed to the hyper-progressive innovators in Berkeley, but it also provided a proof point that caught the attention of early adopters, who began to develop visions for how to expand the market nationally.

As you consider how to move a market and address the barrier to a population adopting a change, a bright spot might be something already happening and just needing amplification, or it may be something you need to create, as Alice Waters did.

In our case study on vegetarian diets from the previous chapter, what are the bright spots that would overcome barriers to your target adoption segment dropping animals from their diet? What would they need to see or experience to make the change? For example, my father-in-law was shocked when he had a vegetarian meal that was both delicious and filling. That meal was a bright spot that didn't turn him into a vegetarian, but it did overcome his perception that you can't have a good meal without meat.

2. Research & Data

Research is most often a tool to help create incremental shifts in a field, but it can also become a much more powerful lever. In the context of the Purpose Economy, research can provide insights that inspire entrepreneurs to pursue markets as innovators. And, given that the Purpose Economy isn't only about the bottom line, research often defines how to measure non-financial success. In this context, new research or data that changes how you think about success in a market can fundamentally shift the entire market. As consumers, we see this all the time in new medical research that changes our understanding of what foods we should be eating more or less of.

As referenced in the last chapter, there is already significant research on the medical challenges created by eating animals, as well as the environmental impact. What additional research could change or remove barriers to people making the change? What perceptions do the target adoption segment carry around with them that prevents them from making the switch? What beliefs are they holding that need debunking? For example, what are their beliefs about the health benefits of animal products that might make them believe they need meat to be healthy and strong?

3. Disruptive Technology

Disruptive technology can include everything from new medicine to mobile applications. Like bright spots, it changes our understanding of what is possible and gives markets new tools to advance their growth. The most disruptive technologies, such as the polio vaccine, can catalyze massive change. Information technology has certainly been doing this, with examples popping up all the time, from classics like WebMD to mobile applications that help organize responses to disasters.

You likely saw the recent headlines about a technology that might disrupt the vegetarian diet market. In August of 2013, the first in vitro beef burger, created by a Dutch team, was eaten at a demonstration for the press in London.[12] It was an animal-flesh product that had never been part of a living animal. It isn't a technology that is yet cost-effective or scalable, and it certainly raises ethical issues, but it exemplifies how a disruptive technology might impact the vegetarian market.

4. Public Perception

People are unlikely to join a market if they don't know about it or have the wrong frame of mind about it. A great deal can be accomplished by changing public consciousness. For example, a series of health-related marketing campaigns by former New York City mayor Michael Bloomberg has brought about dramatic changes in the largest city in the United States, such as the ban on indoor smoking, and has led to the adoption of similar laws in other cities and countries.

Another issue is the hot topic of the death penalty. For several decades, American support for the death penalty was strong and growing. People bought into the mindset of 'an eye for an eye', and despite many campaigns to try to change perception, nothing seemed to work. The Innocence Project, which uses new DNA testing technology, showed that there were people on death row who were actually innocent. They reframed the issue to appeal to Americans' fear of executing innocent people. For many, the injustice of a criminal not getting executed was lesser than the risk of executing someone innocent. This simple reframing began to turn the tide for public perception of the death penalty in America.

For our case study on the vegetarianism market, what public perceptions need to change to spur the next adoption segment to make the move? What perceptions do they hold that are preventing them from taking action? What do they need to experience in order to change? For example, if they saw firsthand the inside of a slaughterhouse, would that alter their perceptions about eating meat? The livestock and dairy industries seem to think so and have moved to prevent the public and media from being to able to see the animal production process.

5. Policy

When you change policy, which most often means changing public policy, you change the rules of the market. Companies and special interest groups know the power of changing laws and government buying behavior in a market. Changes in corporate policies can also have significant impact. Many companies have such a large footprint that when they change their purchasing or hiring policies, for example, they can quickly move a market forward.

City Year changed policy to create and fund AmeriCorps, which enables 80,000 people per year to serve in their community. Walmart began to push their suppliers to provide sustainable products, which began to change how hundreds of companies made products.

Are there changes in corporate or government policies that would impact the adoption of vegetarianism? The government could outlaw animal consumption, but that is neither likely nor necessary to get the next segment of the adoption curve to change. What incentives are companies and governments making for people to continue to consume animal products? How are they impacting pricing and public perception? These are the kinds of questions that would likely uncover a strategy to put policy to work for the current market.

The Levers in Action: Building the Pro Bono Market

These five market levers can and often should be employed in combination. In my work with the Taproot Foundation, we used all five over a dozen years, although out of the gate, my focus was on creating a bright spot. Pro bono service had unfortunately acquired a reputation as being both unreliable and unable to scale—most nonprofits had given up on it.

To realize my vision of empowering all nonprofits with pro bono service, it was clear that I had to begin by showing what was possible. The benchmark from my scan of the field was that less than 50 percent of pro bono projects were completed, and that the largest pro bono programs were delivering services to only a few dozen nonprofits. These poor outcomes had built a perception among nonprofits that pro bono is a waste of time. Taproot would need to significantly surpass those numbers if we wanted to prove that something different was possible.

It took us just over five years, but we did it. By leveraging best practices from a wide range of industries, including Costco's product development and pricing methods, Deloitte's consulting model, and the nomenclature of the most effective charitable foundations, we were able to achieve a 95 percent completion rate and scale to hundreds of projects a year. Our **bright spot** caught the attention of the field, and soon, new pro bono programs were popping up all over the world. We had done more than just serve nonprofits: we created scale and credibility for the market, which attracted new entrepreneurs and capital.

Leveraging the success created by our bright spot, Taproot shifted its focus to **policy.** We never worked to change government policy; our focus instead was to change corporate volunteer policies. These were the organizations that would create the rulebook for our market, and we needed them to shift their policies to open up the market. To get them to do that, we knew we needed to move them away from measuring the success of corporate volunteerism by quantity of hours devoted by their employees (which had been the norm), to measuring success by the quality of work done.

While we didn't work to change public policy, we did find one of our most valuable and most needed allies in the highest seat in government. Thus far in our pursuit of changing the way people think about pro bono, perhaps no single achievement is quite as large-scale as the White House's embrace of the mission. The day

I heard President George W. Bush say the words "pro bono" in a speech, I knew we were nearing a tipping point. The President had publicly gotten behind our vision and was challenging American businesses to embrace pro bono service. He had begun to change **public perception**.

Roughly a year earlier, I met with Nancy Murphy, who was then leading the CSR practice at APCO Worldwide and serving on our board. She explained that APCO had been hired to help advise the President's Council on Service and Civic Participation, led by Jean Case. It was populated with leaders from nearly every walk of life, including a NASCAR driver, corporate leaders, the president of the University of Texas, and the head coach of the Indianapolis Colts. It was a star-studded production, but as Nancy explained, they had one major problem: there was no strategy for how to use their platform to create meaningful change in the country.

Nancy put the question to me directly: If I could have this council and the President get behind a campaign, what would it look like? I shared with her the story about the role of President John F. Kennedy in creating the modern pro bono ethic in the legal profession. In 1962, JFK had called a summit of the leading attorneys around the nation. He urged this powerful group of legal minds to ensure that the new civil rights laws that had just passed were enforced. JFK knew that while he had won the battle in D.C., the war would be won or lost in the courtrooms. Success would require an army of pro bono legal support, he told the lawyers, and he asked them to be his civil rights army. Not only did they win the war, but in so doing, they created the modern practice of pro bono service in the legal profession. They turned this great moment of pride for the profession into a core part of the very identity of those who practice law.

Taproot needed a watershed campaign like this for the business community. In an era when the government's role in so many social services was receding, the President needed to call on businesses, in order that the nonprofit sector would be set up to serve our society. This would be an ideal charge for the council and the President, I told Nancy. Gather the leaders of the business professions, and have the President challenge them to pledge pro bono support for the nonprofit sector. Ask them to collectively pledge over a billion dollars in pro bono. It wasn't the $200 billion needed, but it could be the spark to catalyze the establishment of pro bono as a field.

Jean Case loved the idea and embraced it as her own. The group developed "A Billion + Change" as a multi-year campaign, and it became the core focus of the council. While it hit a few speed bumps along the way, the campaign would eventually surpass $2 billion in pledges from companies and transcend the Bush administration to continue under President Obama.

In addition, Taproot made use of the lever of **research and data** in growing the pro bono market on an annual basis. The most powerful examples came through our work to overcome the perception of many nonprofits that pro bono was only for unsuccessful nonprofits that couldn't afford to pay. We studied the highest profile and top-performing nonprofits in the country and found that with very few exceptions, they relied on pro bono services for 10 to 20 percent of their budgets. Pro bono was a necessary ingredient for success, not a desperate option for failing nonprofits. This research began to change perception in the nonprofit sector about the importance of pro bono service.

Disruptive technology also proved key in building the pro bono market. When we first opened an office in New York City, I met with Brooke Mahoney, then the head of the Volunteer Consulting Group. Her organization was widely respected in the city for its efforts to engage business professionals in work for nonprofits. Sitting in her office with a PowerPoint presentation, I shared our service grant model with her, and she dismissed it out of hand. "It isn't possible," she said. "I tried it ten years ago and it didn't work. It was too expensive and took way too much staff time to manage."

It was an interesting moment as an entrepreneur, highlighting the good fortune I had in starting the Taproot Foundation when I did, back in 2001. Brooke had had basically the same notion, but she had failed ten years earlier, because the technology didn't exist to make the idea possible. Since then, the Internet and the widespread use of email had changed the nature of what could be done virtually. It had disrupted the way we work and had made working in a virtual team and managing a virtual program possible. Even simple tools like online group emails and free conference calling services made the difference between the service grant model working or failing, as it had earlier.

Roughly ten years later, technology once again played a critical role in advancing the pro bono marketplace. In about 2009, I began receiving emails from colleagues about a woman who was creating a new pro bono program. A few months later, someone finally sent me a link to her website, Catchafire, a company that matched nonprofits with individual pro bono consultants to do predefined capacity building projects. The business model was based on a matching fee that Catchafire charged nonprofits for the service.

Rachael Chong and I finally met, and I loved what she was doing. In fact, she had been inspired by Taproot, but she didn't like the model. As a junior investment banker, Rachael didn't have the time to do a service grant, and we didn't need the skills she had to offer. That is, she liked the idea but thought the execution was wrong. With Catchafire, volunteers would work solo, rather than in teams, and the time commitment would be 50 hours, not a hundred. The experience would also be largely online, to avoid the cost and inconvenience of coordinating in person interactions. It could be a much more scalable solution. We had created a Costco, and she had designed something closer to Amazon.com, offering a large catalog of small solutions with online payment.

Taproot's most recent partnership harnesses the power of one of the most successful technological innovations in recent years—the remarkable reach and connectedness of LinkedIn. LinkedIn's goal is to connect talent with opportunity. The logical extension was to connect their 250 million members with opportunities to create an impact—to do pro bono work.

Operating as an action tank, Taproot was able to identify barriers to adoption and then work to remove them by using the five levers. Combined, the diffusion of innovations framework and the five levers created a powerful model any leader could deploy to change the world, one market at a time.

Five Levers in Action: Nine Mini-Case Studies

You can find these levers in action across industries and sectors. While Taproot used all five, different organizations moved markets by using different levers.

1. Mosaic: Solar Energy

Mosaic, an online portal for solar energy investment and crowdsourced finance, utilized disruptive energy and financing sector technologies to address the public perception of solar's high investment costs. Publicly subsidizing solar investments has been tricky from a policy perspective, but Mosaic's decision  to crowdsource its financing and "green" investment was not only a clever marketing tool, but another way to challenge perceptions of the business viability of solar energy. To date, $5.6 million has been invested through the Mosaic platform.

2. OMEGA: Biofuels

The OMEGA (Offshore Membrane Enclosures for Growing Algae) Project used new research and data by scientists and engineers to create a disruptive technology in the form of algae.

Unlike most algae, OMEGA's algae works as both a biofuel and "cleaner" that doesn't feed on ecosystem resources, such as food, fertilizer, or land. Furthermore, the combination of both emerging research and disruptive technology creates the opportunity for others in the field to develop even further. While this  worked as a controlled pilot project, the next step is to understand the commercial viability of offshore OMEGA systems for a variety of uses, including biofuels production, wastewater treatment, and carbon sequestration.

3. Kickstarter: Crowdsourced Investment

Kickstarter, an online platform for crowdfunding independent creative projects, launched in 2009 using secure online fundraising platforms (itself a recent disruptive technology). The platform recognized and filled a gap for creative entrepreneurs, designers, and other freelancers wanting to maintain  creative control over their projects. The founders like to highlight this process as being rooted in the time of Mozart or Mark Twain, who solicited money from their communities and gave that community one of their finished products. Even so, Kickstarter's inventive use of technology to harness the power of the creative community has enabled a crowd-sourced $789 million for 53,672 different projects, and in the process, Kickstarter has become one of the most influential bright spots in and beyond the tech world.

4. B Lab: Responsible Business Leadership

B Lab began with the vision of "redefining success in business". They leveraged the bright spot of social enterprise by creating infrastructure to help scale what were mostly grassroots efforts into a new organizational structure. But their most meaningful accomplishment may be their success in lobbying 19 states (as of this writing) to pass legislation that legally recognizes a new, socially responsible corporate structure—the Benefit Corporation.

5. Khan Academy: Open Education

The Khan Academy emerged as MOOCs (massive open online courses) and began making headlines. Like other MOOCs, Khan Academy used technology—the Internet and its myriad media and sharing channels—to disrupt the education space. However, in offering online courses for free, Khan was able to tackle the lack of access to good, quality, public education in a way that garnered incredible support very early on at little cost. Leveraging this early success, Khan gained the financial backing and support needed to pioneer and launch the first "elementary" MOOC of its kind. Today, Khan Academy reaches about 10 million students per month and has delivered over 300 million lessons.

6. Fair Trade USA: Fair Trade Consumer Products

The Fair Trade movement is rooted in a growing sentiment that the food consumers and suppliers purchase should be produced in conditions that are safe, with wages that are fair, using practices that are sustainable to the environment and the communities they impact. This sentiment arises from disconcerting research and news reports. The simple stamp of approval, a "fair trade certified" Fair Trade USA icon (which can now be found on over 12 thousand products in 100 thousand U.S. retail locations), was effectively a campaign for more humane production

methods and practices. This tactic has helped change public perceptions around ethical means of production. Leveraging these changing public perceptions, the group created a foundation that is now a vehicle for affecting policy, creating awareness, supporting transparency, and promoting best practices in the supply chain.

7. San Francisco Public Utility Commission: Utility Conservation

The San Francisco Public Utility Commission is exemplary among American utility providers. Buttressed by public perception, policy, research, and new, renewable technologies, the Commission decided not merely to begin to incorporate sustainable technology and energy into their portfolio of provi-

sions. They also made it their imperative and mission to consider the environment and community interests as their priority for all water, power, and sewage provision. By creating a new bright spot for other monopolistic companies to imitate, SFPUC has helped move the needle for the industry. Pulling from a 1987 Brundtland Report (*Our Common Future*) on Sustainable Development, they define their groundbreaking journey with "development that meets the needs of the present without compromising the ability of future generations to meet their own needs."

8. Freelancers Union: Independent Workforce

In 1995, the Freelancers Union (originally named Working Today) was founded in New York City in order to represent the needs and concerns of the growing independent workforce. The organization uses compelling research and campaigns to find innovative ways to bring together and support its 380,000  members and the country's 42 million independent workers. Modeled in part after the AARP, the Freelancers Union offers health insurance to its membership. In the past few years, the organization has opened up an innovative health clinic for its members in Brooklyn and fought successfully for policy change in New York City to eliminate the unincorporated business tax for independent workers—a move that saves its members up to $3,400 annually.

9. Practice Fusion: Health Care Transparency

Practice Fusion is an electronic health record (EHR) company that distinguished itself from a crowded field of health tech companies by pioneering an innovative, free, web-based model for EHR technology. As one of the nation's largest and fastest growing health care platforms, Practice Fusion has leveraged  a disruptive technology to show both patients and practitioners that EHR can create greater fluidity and transparency by putting the patient at the center of care.

Which Market Will You Change?

So, what steps do you need to take as you create your Purpose Economy organization with the action tank model in mind?

Action Tank Checklist

Step One: Define Your Market

What is a market (i.e. need and opportunity) you seek to move?

☐ Need and/or problem is defined.
☐ Opportunity or key insight to address the need is defined.

Test your market definition:
☐ It is specific (i.e. not world peace)

☐ It is well-defined and bound/discrete (e.g. geography, population, or demographic)

☐ Motivation should be clear (i.e. why does it matter to you?)

☐ Doesn't assume a solution (i.e. is it forcing one solution?)

Step Two: Select a Metric to Measure Progress

What is the single metric that will determine if the market is moving?

☐ Metric is defined.

Test your metric:
☐ It can be realistically measured

☐ It is likely largely causal or just one of many variables

☐ Using the metric wouldn't influence your strategy negatively (i.e. create counter-productive incentives to game the metric)

☐ It is ideally further bound by geography or demographic definition

☐ Significant change would likely take 5 to 10 years (not too much earlier or later)

Step Three: Identify Your Target Audience

Who is the target audience for the action tank?

☐ Defined the population you want to change.

Test your target population:
☐ Is this the audience that needs to adopt new behavior to create the change (e.g. real estate developers are those that need to change to address affordable housing, not residents)?

☐ Is there an 80/20 rule you can apply to focus the effort (e.g. decrease drunk driving incidents, so focus on teenagers)?

☐ Identified the latest segment on the adoption curve to have adopted the change.
☐ Defined which segment is your target and is the next to adopt.

Test your adoption segment:
- ☐ Is this audience not already engaged in the market?

- ☐ Is the segment before it already fully engaged?

- ☐ Top barriers for your adoption segment to change are defined.

Test your barriers:
- ☐ Are these barriers largely unique to your target audience (i.e. not the other segments along the adoption curve)?

Step Four: Select Levers to Address Barriers

Which of the five levers could best address the barriers you identified?

- ☐ Defined levers to use to address barriers.
- ☐ Mapped your assumptions about why you chose those levers.

Test the levers:
- ☐ Is there any easier way to move the target audience?

- ☐ Project the impact on your metric if you were to pull these levers. Would be it be sufficient?

When It All Comes Together

We were 9,400 feet above sea level, surrounded by walls of mountains, at the Elk Mountain Lodge, a short ride out of Aspen, Colorado—one of the most beautiful places on Earth. It was October, and the aspen trees were golden with the sunset dancing off their leaves.

On that day, that place was the most beautiful because of the woman standing beside me, in a dress as white as the mountaintops.

When I define success, I recall this moment in my life.

I had founded Taproot three years earlier. We were still a young organization and weren't operating anywhere but San Francisco at the time, much less supporting organizations replicating our model around the world. We had delivered less than 10 percent of the $100 million in services to nonprofits that we would by our tenth year. We had engaged only a few hundred of the thousands of professionals who would eventually join our ranks, and we were not yet working with any of the dozens of Fortune 200 companies that would become close partners. I had yet to even conceive of the White House campaign to generate over $2 billion in pro bono services for the community.

In starting the Taproot Foundation, I did something that scared the hell out of me. I left a well-paying job with next to no savings, to do something my executive coach at the time called unrealistic at best. There was no clear way to fund Taproot, and the core concept ran counter to many of the established rules and best practices in the field.

But I could see it, taste it, and smell it. It had to be done. From my experience working in the nonprofit sector, I knew the mission was critical to the future of charitable organizations. From my experience working in product development, I knew that it was technically possible, and that business professionals were not just hungry for purpose, but starving for it. I had found a calling. It wasn't a business plan, an idea, or an organization—it was me. It was an authentic and full representation of who I am as a person and a professional.

Pursuing the vision was a constant high. The early setbacks and the concerns of friends and family only fueled the high and determination. I felt like I'd suddenly been invested with a super power. Rather than a radioactive bug, however, the source of my newfound power was something deep inside me that had been released when I connected with a vision that was profoundly personal and important to me.

My super power certainly didn't grant me any new physical abilities, like leaping from buildings in a single bound (my vertical leap remained at about three inches). But it did something much more meaningful; it allowed me to surround myself with amazing people. I'd even met Kara through the work. She had been an early target for the emerging board of directors (as the joke goes, I over-recruited). Though I had dated a number of wonderful women over the previous ten years, with Kara it was different. Starting Taproot required me to become open to the world and to express myself fully. It had enabled me to find the woman of my dreams and to put my whole self into the relationship in a way that had previously eluded me.

On that cold October day, standing before Kara and me was Dick Matgen, our officiant and one of the most impressive human beings you could ever have the honor to meet. Dick and I had met less than two years previously, when I visited his office at the Peninsula Community Foundation, seeking support for Taproot. He helped us secure our first grant, a $10,000 check that felt like all the money in the world at the time. A former Catholic priest, Dick had left the clergy when he came out. His partner, George, sat in the audience.

With George was Caroline Barlerin and her new husband, Hunter Walk, as well as many old friends, quite a few of whom had become closer over the last few years. They had, in myriad ways, helped me realize my dream; like me, they were part of something bigger than any one of us alone.

Looking at my bride, Dick, Caroline, and the rest of the crew assembled on that cool but stunning October day, I realized that in founding Taproot, I had found myself.

Conclusion

I grew up in a BuJew (parents of Jewish descent practicing Tibetan Buddhism) household and was exposed to the values and traditions of both cultures. I spent my early school years at a Buddhist school, and my parents centered their lives around the Sangha (Buddhist community). They were both of Jewish descent but had found the need to find their own path in the 1960s.

The Jewish concept of *tikkun olam*, a Hebrew phrase that means "repair the world," suggests humanity's shared responsibility to heal, repair, and transform the world. The Tibetan Buddhist tradition's Bodhisattva Vow similarly focuses on repairing the world through the elimination of human suffering. The vow states: "Although beings are numberless, I vow to save them all from suffering. I vow not to attain enlightenment until all beings are free from suffering."

Talk about ambition—repairing the world and saving every being from suffering. But this is ultimately our goal, and we must constantly set it as our true north. That said, both are brilliantly grounded ideas. In setting such unobtainable goals, we also directly have to admit that we will never achieve them, which grounds us in reality and forces us to bring humility to our ambitions within the Purpose Economy.

Glossary

action tank: An effort inside or between organizations that sets goals, identifies the largest barriers to achieving those goals, and takes action to remove those barriers; a more action-oriented version of the think tank.

Agrarian Economy: An economy centered around farming and the land.

Benefit Corporation (B Corp): A corporate form in the U.S. designed for for-profit entities that want to consider society and the environment in addition to profit in their decision making process. B Corps differ from traditional corporations in regards to their purpose, accountability, and transparency.

bright spots: One of the five levers that can be used to move a market in the Purpose Economy, this lever is typically an effort, usually small-scale, that has achieved a remarkable result and can act as starting place for others to build or expand a market.

calling: A psychological approach to work that experiences work and life as seamless. It is most commonly influenced by the psychological approach modeled by parents. See also **career** and **job**.

career: A psychological approach to work that defines work as core to self-esteem and success relative to peers. It is most commonly influenced by the psychological approach modeled by parents. See also **calling** and **job**.

community organizing: The process of identifying, recruiting, and developing leadership, building community around that leadership, and building power out of that community to create meaningful change.

disruptive technology: One of the five levers that can be used to move a market in the Purpose Economy, this lever can change our understanding of what is possible and give markets new tools to advance their growth through the use of new technology.

diffusion of innovations: Theory created by Everett Rogers explaining how, why, and at what rate new ideas and technologies spread through culture. The adoption of innovation is inherently social in nature.

economic evolution: The emergent nature of economies in which each new dominant economy grows out of the foundation of the prior dominant economy. However, instead of displacing the prior economy, the new economy complements and builds from it, serving human needs in distinctive new ways.

five levers for social change: The only five ways to move a market in the Purpose Economy. The five levers are research and data, policy, public perception, disruptive technology, and bright spots.

Gross Domestic Product (GDP): The market value of all officially recognized final goods and services produced within a country in a given period of time. GDP per capita is often considered an indicator of a country's standard of living.

job crafting: A process for reimagining your work life which involves redefining your job to incorporate your motives, strengths, and passions. This exercise prompts you to visualize the job, map its elements, and reorganize them to better suit you.

job: A psychological approach to work that frames work as a means to enable life outside work. It is most commonly influenced by the psychological approach modeled by parents. See also **career** and **calling**.

human-centered design: A process that has been used for decades to create new solutions to design challenges. The process helps people hear the needs of the people and communities they're designing for, create innovative approaches to meet these needs, and deliver solutions that work in specific cultural and economic contexts.

human-scale: An urban design term meaning a manageable scale based on solid understanding and appreciation of community and livability. This scale can be measured qualitatively or quantitatively.

Industrial Economy: A post-Industrial Revolution economy driven by the use of technology to enable increased production of material goods, supporting a larger population with a high capacity for divisions of labor.

Information Economy: An economy with an increased emphasis on informational activities and information industry. The Information Economy as we know it began emerging in earnest in the 1950s. New technologies formed the infrastructure of the Information Economy, culminating with the evolution of the Internet.

market: A cluster of activity in an economy centered around the adoption of specific good, service or behavior change.

Millennial: A person reaching young adulthood around the year 2000. Also known as Generation Y, this demographic cohort is most often referring to people born from the early 1980s to the early 2000s.

policy: One of the five levers that can be used to move a market in the Purpose Economy, the policy lever is typically used to change the rules of the game. It is most often used to describe efforts to change corporate or government policies that impact a market.

pro bono: A Latin phrase meaning "for the public good". Today, it is used to describe professional work undertaken voluntarily and without payment or at a reduced fee as a public service.

public perception: One of the five levers that can be used to move a market in the Purpose Economy, this lever provides a population a new way of thinking about a market, changing consciousness, and reframing an issue to catalyze social change.

purpose: The reason for which something is done or created, or for which something exists. In the case of the Purpose Economy, purpose goes beyond serving others and the planet and also indicates the search for a sense of community and the opportunity for self-expression and personal development.

Purpose Economy: The emerging economy defined by the quest for people to have more purpose in their lives. It is an economy where value creation is focused on enabling purpose for employees and customers—through serving needs greater than their own, enabling personal growth, and building community.

purpose pattern: A way of classifying how people find purpose and fulfillment in their work based upon who they serve, how they serve them, and why they serve them. It is most powerfully expressed as a personal mission or purpose statement.

research: One of the five levers that can be used to move a market in the Purpose Economy, this lever, driven by data and often found in academic settings, can provide insights that inspire leaders and entrepreneurs to change their understanding of a market.

sharing: The joint use of a resource or space.

social capital: A person's relationships and the benefits he or she sees from these relationships; the expected collective or economic benefits derived from the preferential treatment and cooperation between individuals and groups.

social impact: The effect of an activity on the social fabric of the community and well-being of the individuals, families, and society.

social media: Interactions among people in which they create, share, and/or exchange information and ideas in virtual communities and networks.

well-being: The condition of an individual or group, for example, their social, economic, psychological, spiritual, or medical state; the state of being happy, healthy, or successful.

Endnotes

Introduction

1. Hurst, Aaron. "Five Levers for Social Change: Part 1." *Stanford Social Innovation Review.* N.p., 20 Feb. 2012. Web.

SECTION ONE: WELCOME TO THE PURPOSE ECONOMY

Chapter 1: The Purpose Economy

1. "Does Life Need Meaning? CSU Tackles Ultimate Query." *The Denver Post.* N.p., n.d. Web. 01 Jan. 2012. <http://www.denverpost.com/lifestyles/ci_19754476>.

Chapter 2: Economic Evolution

1. Porat, Marc. *The Information Economy: Definition and Measurement.* Rep. Washington, D.C: Superintendent of Documents, U.S. Government Printing Office, 1977. *Eric.ed.gov.* Web.

2. Porat, Marc. *The Information Economy.* Excerpt from Ambrosi, Alain, Valérie Peugeot and Daniel Pimienta, eds. *Word Matters: multicultural perspectives on information societies.* N.p., Nov. 2005. Web.

3. "Employee Tenure Summary." *U.S. Bureau of Labor Statistics.* U.S. Bureau of Labor Statistics, 18 Sept. 2012. Web.

4. Hartung, Paul and Taber, Brian. "1. Career Construction: Heeding the Call of the Heart." In Bryan J. Dik, Zinta S. Byrne, and Michael F. Steger, eds. *Purpose and Meaning in the Workplace.* Washington, D.C: American Psychological Association, 2013. Print.

5. "Gross Domestic Product by Selected Industries and State: 2009." *Gross Domestic Product (GDP).* N.p., 2009. Web.

6. "The 2011 Statistical Abstract." *Gross Domestic Product (GDP).* United States Census Bureau, 2011. Web.

7. "The 2012 Statistical Abstract." *Gross Domestic Product (GDP).* United States Census Bureau, 2012. Web.

8. Sutton, Mark. "Social Media Revenue to Reach $16.9bn." *Http://www.itp.net.* N.p., n.d. Web. 13 Sept. 2013.

9. "The Rise of the Sharing Economy." *The Economist.* 9 Mar. 2013. N.p. Web.

10. Larsen, Janet. "Plan B Updates." *Earth Policy Institute.* N.p., 25 Apr. 2013. Web.

11. Frier, Sarah. "Etsy Tops $1 Billion in 2013 Product Sales on Mobile Lift." *Bloomberg.com.* 12 Nov. 2013. Web.

12. "Navigant Research." *Navigant Research*. N.p., n.d. Web.

13. "SelectUSA." *The Energy Industry in the United States*. N.p., n.d. Web. 08 Nov. 2013.

Chapter 3: The Ten Drivers of the New Economy

1. "Infographic: Freelance Revolution in America—1.7 Million Job Openings in 2011 and Counting." *PRWeb*. N.p., 26 Oct. 2011. Web.

2. Anders, George. "The 20 Most Desired Employers: From Google to Nike, Accenture." *Forbes*. 11 Oct. 2012. Web.

3. Grant, Adam. "What Millennials Really Want Out of Work." *LinkedIn*. N.p., n.d. Web. 01 Aug. 2013.

4. "The Millennials: Confident. Connected. Open to Change." *Pew Research Center RSS*. N.p., 24 Feb. 2010. Web.

5. Wrzesniewski, Amy. "'It's Not Just a Job': Shifting Meanings of Work in the Wake of 9/11." *Journal of Management Inquiry*, 11.3 (2002): 230-34. Print.

6. "Life Expectancy in the USA, 1900-98." *Life Expectancy in the USA, 1900-98*. Demographics Berkeley. N.d. Web.

7. "Encore Careers—Purpose, Passion and a Paycheck in Your Second Act." *Encore.org*. N.p., n.d. Web.

8. "Trip Tracker Program." *Boulder Valley School District*. N.p., n.d. Web.

9. Jacobs, Deborah L. "Charitable Giving: Baby Boomers Donate More, Study Shows." *Forbes*. 08 Aug. 2013. Web.

10. "Baby Boomers and Volunteering: Findings from Corporation Research." N.p., Mar. 2007. Web. <*http://www.nationalservice.gov/sites/default/files/documents/boomer_research.pdf*>.

11. "International Human Development Indicators—United Nations Development Programme." *International Human Development Indicators*. N.p., n.d. Web.

12. "Traditional Families Account for Only 7 Percent of U.S. Households." *Population Reference Bureau*. N.p., Mar. 2003. Web.

13. "U.S. Bureau of Economic Analysis." *U.S. Bureau of Economic Analysis*. N.p., n.d. Web. 11 June 2012.

14. "Occupational Employment Projections to 2020." *Bureau of Labor Statistics*. N.p., Jan. 2012. Web.

15. "Administration on Aging." *Administration on Aging*. N.p., n.d. Web.

16. "U.S. Bureau of Labor Statistics." *U.S. Bureau of Labor Statistics*. N.d. Web.

17. "Babysitters, Nannies, Child Care and Senior Home Care." *Care.com*. N.d. Web.

18. Seligman, Martin E. P. *Flourish: A Visionary New Understanding of Happiness and Well-being*. New York: Free, 2011. Print.

19. Grant, Adam M. *Give and Take: A Revolutionary Approach to Success*. New York, NY: Viking, 2013. Print.

20. Friedman, Thomas L. *The World Is Flat: A Brief History of the Twenty-first Century*. New York: Farrar, Straus and Giroux, 2005. Print.

21. Harth, Chris. "GSF Fact Sheet 1: The State of Global Studies in the United States." Publication, Global Studies Foundation. N.d. Web.

22. Gardner, John W. *Self-Renewal: The Individual and the Innovative Society*. New York: Norton, 1981. Print.

23. "Public Trust in Government: 1958-2013." *Pew Research Center for the People and the Press RSS*. N.p., 18 Oct. 2013. Web.

24. "Partisan Polarization Surges in Bush, Obama Years." *Pew Research Center for the People and the Press RSS*. N.p., 4 June 2012. Web.

25. "The 2008 Statistical Abstract." *Gross Domestic Product (GDP)*. United States Census Bureau, 2008. Web.

26. "The 2009 Statistical Abstract." *Gross Domestic Product (GDP)*. United States Census Bureau, 2009. Web.

27. "B Corporation." *B Corporation*. N.p., n.d. Web.

SECTION TWO: PERSONAL PURPOSE—OWNING IT

Chapter 4: Purpose Is What Matters

1. Thompson, Derek. "The New Economics of Happiness." *The Atlantic*. N.p., 23 May 2012. Web.

2. Seligman, Martin E.P. "Authentic Happiness: Using the New Positive Psychology." *Authentic Happiness*. N.p., Apr. 2011. Web.

3. Senior, Jennifer. "All Joy and No Fun: Why Parents Hate Parenting." *NYMag.com*. N.p., 4 July 2010. Web.

4. Gardner, John W. *Self-Renewal: The Individual and the Innovative Society*. New York: Norton, 1981. Print.

5. Brooks, Arthur C. "A Formula for Happiness." *The New York Times*. N.p., 14 Dec. 2013. Web.

Chapter 5: Purpose Myth-Busting

1. Stern, Ken. "Why the Rich Don't Give to Charity." *The Atlantic*. N.p., 20 Mar. 2013. Web. 21 Dec. 2013.

2. "General Social Survey." *General Social Survey*. N.p., n.d. Web.

3. Bellah, Robert N. *Habits of the Heart: Individualism and Commitment in American Life*. Berkeley: University of California, 1985. Print.

4. Wrzesniewski, Amy. "Jobs, Careers, and Callings. People's Relations to Their Work." *Journal of Research in Personality*, 31 (1997): 21-33. Web.

5. Staw, B. M., Bell, N. E., & Clausen, J. A. (1986). "The dispositional approach to job attitudes." *Administrative Science Quarterly*, 31, 56–77.

Staw, B. M., & Ross, J. (1985). "Stability in the midst of change: A dispositional approach to job attitudes." *Journal of Applied Psychology*, 70, 469–480.

6. Berg, Justin M., Amy Wrzesniewski, and Jane E. Dutton. "Perceiving and Responding to Challenges in Job Crafting at Different Ranks: When Proactivity Requires Adaptivity." *Journal of Organizational Behavior* 31, 2-3 (2010): 158-86. Print.

Chapter 6: The WHO, HOW & WHY of Purpose

1. "Google Says GPA Is Worthless (SATs and Brainteasers, Too)." *Wall Street Oasis*. N.p., 21 June 2013. Web.

2. Gardner, Howard. *Responsibility at Work: How Leading Professionals Act (or Don't Act) Responsibly*. San Francisco: Jossey-Bass, 2007. Print.

3. Haidt, Jonathan. "The Moral Foundations of Occupy Wall Street." *Reason.com*. N.p., 20 Oct. 2011. Web.

4. Haidt, Jonathan. "What the Tea Partiers Really Want." *The Wall Street Journal*. 16 Oct. 2010. Web.

Chapter 7: The Practice of Purpose

1. Chida, Y. "Positive Psychological Well-being and Mortality: A Quantitative Review of Prospective Observational Studies." *National Center for Biotechnology Information*. U.S. National Library of Medicine, Sept. 2008. Web.

2. Hoffman, Reid, and Ben Casnocha. *The Start-Up of You*. New York: Crown Business, 2012. Print.

3. Baumeister, R.F., & Vohs, K. D. (2002). "The pursuit of meaningfulness in life." In C. R. Snyder and S. J. Lopez, eds. *The Handbook of Positive Psychology*. New York: Oxford University Press. 608-628.

Pratt, M. G., & Ashforth, B. E. (2003). "Fostering meaningfulness in working and meaningfulness at work: An identity perspective." In K. Cameron, J. E. Dutton and R. E. Quinn, eds. *Positive Organizational Scholarship*. San Francisco: Berret-Koehler.

Wrzesniewski, Amy, Jane E. Dutton, and Gelaye Debebe. "Interpersonal Sensemaking and the Meaning of Work." *Research in Organizational Behavior* 25 (2003): 93-135. Elsevier. Web.

4. Emerson, R. M. "Social Exchange Theory." *Annual Review of Sociology*, Vol. 2 (August 1976): 335-362.

5. Berg, Justin M., Amy Wrzesniewski, and Jane E. Dutton. "Perceiving and Responding to Challenges in Job Crafting at Different Ranks: When Proactivity Requires Adaptivity." *Journal of Organizational Behavior* 31.2-3 (2010): 158-86. Print.

SECTION THREE: SOCIAL PURPOSE—THE PURPOSE ECONOMY ORGANIZATION

Chapter 8: The Purpose Economy Organization

1. "2010 Cause Evolution Study." *Cone Communications: Public Relations & Marketing*. 2010. Web.

2. *2011 Executive Summary Deloitte Volunteer IMPACT Survey*. Deloitte Development LLC, 2011. Print. N.p.

Chapter 9: Purposeful Ventures—Five Opportunities

1. Turkle, Sherry. *Alone Together: Why We Expect More from Technology and Less from Each Other*. New York: Basic, 2012. Print.

2. Amanda Palmer. "The Art of Asking." *TED: Ideas Worth Spreading*. N.p., Mar. 2013. Web.

3. "How Many Books Were Published 100 Years Ago As Compared to Today?" *Stuff Nobody Cares About*. N.p., 31 Jan. 2013. Web.

4. "The History of Education in America." *Chesapeake College*. N.p., n.d. Web. <http://www.chesapeake.edu/Library/EDU_101/eduhist_20thC.asp>.

5. "HSLDA | Home Schooling Works!—The Scholastic Achievement and Demographic Characteristics of Home School Students in 1998." *HSLDA*. N.p., 1999. Web.

Chapter 10: Working with Purpose—The Purpose-Driven Professional

1. "Gallup-Healthways Well-Being Index." *Gallup-Healthways Well-Being Index*. N.p., n.d. Web.

2. Crane, Thomas G., and Lerissa Nancy Patrick. *The Heart of Coaching: Using Transformational Coaching to Create a High-performance Culture*. San Diego: FTA, 2002. Print.

3. Rodell, Jessica B. "Finding Meaning through Volunteering: Why Do Employees Volunteer and What Does It Mean for Their Jobs?" *Academy of Management Journal* 56.5 (2013): 274-294. Print.

4. "Infographic: Freelance Revolution in America—1.7 Million Job Openings in 2011 and Counting." *PRWeb*. N.p., 26 Oct. 2001. Web.

Chapter 11: Leading with Purpose

1. Kopp, Wendy. *One Day, All Children...: The Unlikely Triumph of Teach for America and What I Learned Along the Way.* New York: PublicAffairs, 2011. Print.

2. "Trendwatching.com's May 2011 Trend Briefing Covering THE F-FACTOR." *Trendwatching.com*. N.p., May 2011. Web.

3. Bunderson, Stuart J., and Jeffery A. Thompson. "The Call of the Wild: Zookeepers,

Callings, and the Double-edged Sword of Deeply Meaningful Work." *Johnson Graduate School, Cornell University.* 2009. Web.

SECTION FOUR: SOCIETAL PURPOSE—MOVING MARKETS

Chapter 12: Market Movers

1. Moore, Geoffrey A. *Crossing the Chasm: Marketing and Selling High-Tech Products to Mainstream Customers.* New York: Harper Business, 1999. Print.

2. "Whole Foods Market." *Whole Foods Market.* N.p., n.d. Web.

3. "Supermarket Facts: Industry Overview 2012." *Food Marketing Institute.* N.p., 2012. Web.

4. "U.S. Organic Food Market Increases." *Organic Consumers Association.* N.p., n.d. Web.

5. "U.S. Organic Industry Review 2011." *Organic Trade Organization.* N.p., 2011. Web.

6. "Honest Tea—Refreshingly Honest." *Honest Tea.* N.p., n.d. Web.

7. "The Sustainability Consortium." *The Sustainability Consortium.* N.p., n.d. Web.

8. "City Year: Give a Year. Change the World." *City Year.* N.p., n.d. Web.

9. "Vegetarianism in America." *Vegetarian Times.* N.p., 18 Dec. 2013. Web.

10. "Livestock's Long Shadow: Environmental Issues and Options." *Food and Agriculture Organization of the United Nations.* 2006. Web.

11. Campbell, T. Colin, and Thomas M. Campbell. *The China Study: The Most Comprehensive Study of Nutrition Ever Conducted and the Startling Implications for Diet, Weight Loss and Long-term Health.* Dallas, TX: BenBella, 2005. Print.

12. "In Vitro Meat: First Public Trial." *Wikipedia.* Wikimedia Foundation, 17 Dec. 2013. Web.

References

Acuff, Jonathan M. *Start: Punch Fear in the Face, Escape Average, Do Work That Matters.* Brentwood, TN: Lampo, 2013. Print.

Baker, Wayne E. *Achieving Success through Social Capital: Tapping the Hidden Resources in Your Personal and Business Networks.* San Francisco: Jossey-Bass, 2000. Print.

Bishop, Matthew, and Michael Green. *Philanthrocapitalism: How the Rich Can Save the World.* New York: Bloomsbury, 2008. Print.

Block, Peter. *The Answer to How Is Yes: Acting on What Matters.* San Francisco, CA: Berrett-Koehler, 2002. Print.

Bolles, Richard Nelson. *What Color Is Your Parachute?, 2012.* Berkeley, CA: Ten Speed, 2012. Print.

Briscoe, Jon P., Douglas T. Hall, and Wolfgang Mayrhofer. *Careers around the World: Individual and Contextual Perspectives.* New York: Routledge, 2012. Print.

Campbell, T. Colin and Campbell, Thomas. *The China Study.* Dallas, 2004. Print.

Cameron, Kim S., Jane E. Dutton, and Robert E. Quinn. *Positive Organizational Scholarship: Foundations of a New Discipline.* San Francisco, CA: Berrett-Koehler, 2003. Print.

Chatman, J. A. & O'Reilly, C. A. 1994. "Working smarter and harder: A longitudinal study of managerial success." *Administrative Science Quarterly*, 39: 603-627.

Chatman, J. A. 1991. "Matching people and organizations: Selection and socialization in public accounting firms." *Administrative Science Quarterly*, 36: 459-484.

Chesbrough, Henry William., Wim Vanhaverbeke, and Joel West. *Open Innovation: Researching a New Paradigm.* Oxford: Oxford UP, 2006. Print.

Ciulla, Joanne B. *The Working Life: The Promise and Betrayal of Modern Work.* New York: Times, 2000. Print.

Clements, Jeffrey D. *Corporations Are Not People: Why They Have More Rights than You Do and What You Can Do about It.* San Francisco: Berrett-Koehler, 2012. Print.

Collins, James C., and Jerry I. Porras. *Built to Last: Successful Habits of Visionary Companies.* London: Random House, 2005. Print.

Coutu, D. L. "How resilience works." *Harvard Business Review.* May, 2002. Web.

Cross, R. and R.J. Thomas "How top talent uses networks and where rising stars get trapped." *Organizational Dynamics,* 37 (2008): 165-180.

Cross, R. and Prusak, L. "The people that make organizations stop—or go." *Harvard Business Review.* 2002.

Dik, Bryan J., Zinta S. Byrne, and Michael F. Steger. *Purpose and Meaning in the Workplace.* Washington, D C; American Psychological Association, 2013. Print.

Feynman, Richard P. *The Meaning of It All: Thoughts of a Citizen-Scientist.* Reading, MA: Perseus Books, 1998. Print.

Foremski, Tom. "Fortune Asks, 'Why Does America Hate Silicon Valley?'" *ZDNet.* N.p., 4 Oct. 2013. Web.

Freedman, Marc. *Encore: Finding Work That Matters in the Second Half of Life.* New York: PublicAffairs, 2007. Print.

Friedman, Thomas L. *The World Is Flat: A Brief History of the Twenty-first Century.* New York: Farrar, Straus and Giroux, 2005. Print.

Gardner, Howard. *Responsibility at Work: How Leading Professionals Act (or Don't Act) Responsibly.* San Francisco: Jossey-Bass, 2007. Print.

Gardner, John W. *Self-Renewal: The Individual and the Innovative Society.* New York: Norton, 1981. Print.

Gilbert, Daniel Todd. *Stumbling on Happiness.* New York: A.A. Knopf, 2006. Print.

Gini, Al. *My Job, My Self.* New York (N.Y.): Routledge, 2001. Print.

Gladwell, Malcolm. *David and Goliath: Underdogs, Misfits, and the Art of Battling Giants.* New York: Little, Brown & Company, 2013. Print.

Gorrell, Paul, and John Hoover. *The Coaching Connection: A Manager's Guide to Developing Individual Potential in the Context of the Organization.* New York: American Management Association, 2009. Print.

Grant, Adam M. *Give and Take: A Revolutionary Approach to Success.* New York, NY: Viking, 2013. Print.

Hewlett, Sylvia Ann. *Top Talent: Keeping Performance up When Business Is Down.* Boston, MA: Harvard Business, 2009. Print.

Hill, L. "Beyond the myth of the perfect mentor: Building a network of developmental relationships." *Harvard Business Review.* 1991.

Hochschild, Arlie Russell. *The Time Bind.* New York: Owl Books, 2001. Print.

Ibarra, H. and Lineback, K. "What's your story?" *Harvard Business Review.* 2005.

Ibarra, Herminia. *Working Identity: Unconventional Strategies for Reinventing Your Career.* Boston, MA: Harvard Business School, 2003. Print.

Iyengar, S. S., R. E. Wells and B. Schwartz. "Doing better but feeling worse: Looking for the best jobs undermines satisfaction." *Psychological Science*, 17.2 (2006): 143-150.

Kinal, Therese. "The Evolution of Management." *Business Matters*. N.p., 28 May 2013. Web.

Kohn, Melvin L., and Carmi Schooler. "Job Conditions and Personality: A Longitudinal

Assessment of Their Reciprocal Effects." *American Journal of Sociology* 87.6 (1982): 257-289. Print.

Kopp, Wendy. *One Day, All Children...: The Unlikely Triumph of Teach for America and What I Learned Along the Way*. New York: PublicAffairs, 2011. Print.

Lennick, Doug, and Fred Kiel. *Moral Intelligence: Enhancing Business Performance and Leadership Success*. Upper Saddle River, NJ: Wharton School Pub., 2005. Print.

Linton, Ian. "Five Differences Between Service and Manufacturing Organizations." *Small Business*. N.p., n.d. Web.

Lombardo, Michael M., and Robert W. Eichinger. *FYI: For Your Improvement: A Guide for Development and Coaching*.Minneapolis, Minn. Lominger International, 2009. Print.

McCrea, Jennifer, Jeffrey C. Walker, and Karl Weber. *The Generosity Network: New Transformational Tools for Successful Fund-Raising*. New York: Crown, 2013. Print.

McKnight, John, and Peter Block. *The Abundant Community: Awakening the Power of Families and Neighborhoods*. Chicago: American Planning Association, 2010. Print.

Moore, Geoffrey A. *Crossing the Chasm: Marketing and Selling High-tech Products to Mainstream Customers*. New York: HarperBusiness, 1999. Print.

Page, Karen L. and Joel M. Podolny. "Network forms of organization." *Annual Review of Sociology*. 1998.

Pontefract, Dan. *Flat Army: Creating a Connected and Engaged Organization*. Toronto, ON: Jossey-Bass, 2013. Print.

Powell, Walter W. "Neither Market Nor Hierarchy: Network Forms of Organizations." *Research in Organizational Behavior* 12 (1990): 295-336. Print.

Ragins, B. R. and Cotton, J. L. 1999. "Mentor functions and outcomes: A comparison of men and women in formal and informal mentoring relationships." *Journal of Applied Psychology* 84: 529-550.

Roberts, B. W., N. R. Kuncel, R. Shiner, A. Caspi and L. R. Goldberg. "The power of personality: The comparative validity of personality traits, socioeconomic status, and cognitive ability for predicting important life outcomes." *Perspectives on Psychological Science* 2: 313-345.

Ross, Andrew. "No-Collar." *Temple University*. N.p., Aug. 2004. Web.

Salmon, Felix. *Reuters*. N.p., 30 Sept. 2013. Web.

Sandberg, Sheryl, and Nell Scovell. *Lean In: Women, Work, and the Will to Lead*. New York: Alfred A. Knopf, 2013. Print.

Seligman, Martin E. P. *Flourish: A Visionary New Understanding of Happiness and Well-being*. New York: Free, 2011. Print.

Stern, Lewis Richard. *Executive Coaching: Building and Managing Your Professional Practice*. Hoboken, NJ: John Wiley & Sons, 2008. Print.

"Silicon Valley Strategies." *Silicon Valley Strategies*. N.p., n.d. Web.

TED talk: Amanda Palmer

Tennant, Kyle. *Unfriend Yourself: Three Days to Detox, Discern, and Decide about Social Media*. Chicago: Moody, 2012. Print.

"The MBA—some history." *The Economist*. N.p., 17 Oct. 2013. Web.

Thomas, D. A. "The truth about mentoring minorities: Race matters." *Harvard Business Review*. 2001.

Toffler, Alvin. *The Third Wave*. New York: Morrow, 1980. Print.

Turkle, Sherry. *Alone Together: Why We Expect More from Technology and Less from Each Other*. New York: Basic, 2012. Print.

Index

CPSIA information can be obtained at www.ICGtesting.com
Printed in the USA
BVOW02*0022040516

446599BV00001B/1/P